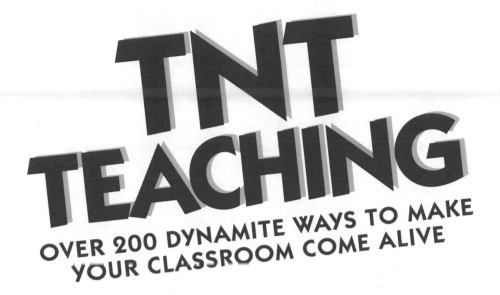

TNT TEACHING

OVER 200 DYNAMITE WAYS TO MAKE YOUR CLASSROOM COME ALIVE

Written and illustrated by Randy Moberg

Edited by Pamela Espeland

free spirit
PUBLiSHiNG®

Works for kids™

DEDICATION

*With all my love, I dedicate this book to my wife, Melissa,
and our three sons, Joshua, Tyler, and Michael.*

*Special thanks go to Pamela Espeland and Judy Galbraith at Free Spirit
and Nancy Tuminelly at MacLean & Tuminelly for helping my dream become a reality.*

*Thanks, too, to my colleagues and students at Osseo Area Schools, District 279,
for their support and inspiration.*

Library of Congress Cataloging-in-Publication Data

Moberg, Randy, 1959–
    TNT teaching : over 200 dynamite ways to make your classroom come alive / written and illustrated by Randy Moberg ; edited by Pamela Espeland.
       p.   cm.
    ISBN 0-915793-64-4
    1. Teaching—Aids and devices. 2. Education, Elementary—Activity programs—United States—Handbooks, manuals, etc. I. Title.
    LB1044.88.M63 1991
    371.3'078—dc20
                                     93-37991
                                               CIP

Cover and book design by MacLean & Tuminelly

10 9 8 7 6 5 4

Printed in the United States of America

FREE SPIRIT PUBLISHING INC.
400 First Avenue North, Suite 616
Minneapolis, MN 55401
(612) 338-2068

DEAR TEACHER,

You and I share a common challenge: how to come up with new ways to teach "the same old stuff"—the basic curriculum that must be presented year after year (after year). We look for novel ways to present fresh material because we want our students to stay interested and excited. The trouble is, we don't always have time to invent or research innovative teaching techniques. We barely have time to do our regular teaching!

Here's help for times when you want to try something new without spending hours and days you don't have. Open this book to practically any page to find suggestions, tips, and ideas to use with your students. Some put a different twist on a straightforward technique you may already use. Others are wacky, outrageous, and off the wall—but go ahead and try them anyway. The look of amazement on your students' faces will make it all worthwhile.

Of course, there is a serious side to even the silliest teaching tool: When it works, our students learn something. That's what we're here for—in front of the class, in our seats or on our feet, year after year.

I can't promise that all of these ideas will work for you, but I can tell you that they have worked for me. They have come directly out of my experience as an elementary school teacher and gifted education specialist. My students seem to enjoy my classes, and their performance indicates that real learning is taking place. Each idea has been tested on real students (mine) in real classrooms.

So scan the contents and flip through the pages until something catches your eye. Then try it out on your class. Many of these techniques require little advance preparation and few or no special materials beyond those you might already have in your classroom on an ordinary day. I wanted to make *TNT Teaching* easy for you to use. I hope it finds a permanent place on your desk or table. I hope it gets dog-eared, beat up, dusty with chalk and full of inky fingerprints.

Good luck and good teaching in your own Free Spirited Classroom,

RANDY MOBERG

JANUARY 1994

CONTENTS

12 WAYS TO MAKE THE MOST OF
TNT TEACHING

1. ***Think of this book as a "fingertip tool."*** When planning your lessons, keep *TNT Teaching* at fingertip distance. It will help you become more creative, resourceful, organized, efficient, and effective. The techniques are designed to work with any age group or subject.

2. ***Cater to your audience.*** Prepare your lessons from your students' vantage point. (The better you know them, the easier this will be.) What are their likes and dislikes? What "turns them on"—and what "turns them off"? Rehearse and experience each lesson in your mind from your students' point of view. Select techniques you think they will enjoy most and benefit from—techniques that will keep them interested and engaged.

3. ***Go for variety.*** Vary your instructional techniques on a regular basis. Keep your students guessing and wondering what will happen next. Shock the senses—the element of surprise is a powerful motivator. You may want to use several techniques in a single lesson, depending on how long it is—and how much energy you have! Add color whenever possible for excitement and stimulation.

4. ***Remember the Law of Diminishing Returns.*** Techniques used repeatedly wear out their welcome. Students lose interest and retain less; motivation takes a nose dive. There are more than 200 different ideas in this book; why limit yourself to the same old three or four? On the other hand....

5. ***Don't get trapped by the Super Teacher Syndrome.*** Teachers in general are very hard workers, spending hours beyond the call of duty preparing lessons and classroom materials. *TNT Teaching* is full of instructional techniques that will make you a better teacher. But don't think you have to incorporate these techniques into *every* lesson *every* day of the week. I'm satisfied if I use just one or two a day—and I wrote the book!

6. ***Feel free to modify and customize.*** These techniques are not written in stone. Use your own creativity, imagination, and inventiveness—and your "inside knowledge" about your students—to make them work in your classroom.

7. ***Have fun.*** Let your inhibitions go and try ideas you've never tried before. Let your students see that you're having a good time. The human spirit can be contagious. This is fun-damental.

8. ***Try, try again.*** If a certain technique doesn't work on a particular day, try it again another time. As teachers, there are so many variables we can't control—behavior problems, group maturity, the time of day, interruptions, and even barometric pressure, which can affect our students' moods and energy levels. There have been times when I've taught the exact same lesson in precisely the same way to different groups, and in each case the outcome has been different. If a technique appeals to you but doesn't seem to reach your students, set it aside to try again later.

9. ***Don't be afraid to look "silly."*** As you read through the techniques in *TNT Teaching,* you may think to yourself, "I could never do that!" or "My students wouldn't respect me." If your teaching has been more formal or traditional up until now, your students may wonder about the change, but I guarantee that they won't respect you any less. And they'll stop wondering as they get caught up in the excitement of your teaching. Students respect—and love—teachers who reach out to them on their level, who laugh with them and clearly enjoy being with them. Think about your favorite teachers. Why did you like them so much? Perhaps because they weren't afraid to let down their guard and try something new.

10. ***Develop a scavenger mentality.*** Garage sales and tag sales, going-out-of-business sales, attics, basements, and school supply rooms are gold mines of great ideas for lesson props and classroom materials. The price is usually right, and often you will find things that will hold your students' interest. Look for old clothes, toys, containers, lamps, suitcases, scarves, kitchen supplies...you get the idea. Once you catch the bug, you'll always be on the lookout for gimmicks and gadgets that will make your lessons fascinating and fun.

11. ***Get organized.*** As you start collecting resources, think "Versatility, Durability, Store-ability, and Accessibility."

   ▶ *Versatility.* As you accumulate props, visuals, and other materials, try to find ones that may be used with a variety of ages and for a variety of subjects.

   ▶ *Durability.* Materials you will want to use over and over again should be built to last. Laminate cards, posters, and game boards; choose durable containers and visuals.

   ▶ *Store-ability.* For most of us teachers, storage can be a problem. As you gather materials, think about how compact you can make them. They should take up the least amount of space possible on your shelf or in your files.

   ▶ *Accessibility.* It's one thing to have a wealth of supplies and props; it's another to be able to put your hands on them quickly. Make yours accessible by categorizing and labeling them, then storing them in a place that's easy to get to and makes sense. I use cardboard filing boxes and shelves. Stick Post-It Notes in your lesson books and plans to remind you of props and materials that have worked for you.

12. ***Share this book with your students.*** Let them use it as a resource while preparing oral reports, displays or other projects. Get them involved by asking them to create some of the props and visuals you will use in your lessons. Or invite them to look through it, then ask, "What do *you* think we should try next?"

I'd like to know how *TNT Teaching* works for you. Which of these techniques are the most successful in your classroom? If you come up with a great new idea, or if you modify or change a technique and find that it makes a world of difference, I'd appreciate hearing from you. Write to me c/o Free Spirit Publishing Inc., 400 First Avenue North, Suite 616, Minneapolis, MN 55401.

To quote my favorite Chinese proverb: *"I hear and I forget; I see and I remember; I do and I understand."* I have found that these techniques create an instant link between hearing, seeing, and doing, increasing my students' retention level. I feel confident that they will do the same for your students. Write and let me know.

BEYOND THE BLACKBOARD

Creative ways to present key ideas, concepts, and lesson materials

1 — WEAR-A-BOARD

Attach a string to a small board or piece of cardboard so you can wear it around your neck. Add visuals and words appropriate to the lesson. Move freely around the room as you present the lesson on your Wear-A-Board. Don't just circle the room; keep your students interested by going to unexpected places or making unpredictable turns.

2 — PORT-A-BOARDS

Laminate or put contact paper on large pieces of poster paper or tagboard. Write on them with dry-erase markers (commonly used on whiteboards). Mount your Port-A-Boards in convenient or unconventional locations around the classroom, such as the inside of cupboard doors. You can even use them outside; simply tie them with twine to the base of a large tree.

3 — SPECIAL DELIVERY

Do you have a remote control car? If not, borrow one from your own children, a neighborhood child, or a student and bring it to class. Write lesson messages or stick props on the car and deliver them to your students to read and share with the class. For a special treat, invite your students to bring their remote control vehicles to class and have a rally. *Example:* Take this opportunity to teach traffic rules and safety.

IT'S A JUNGLE OUT THERE ▶ 4

With a marker, write lesson ideas or questions on different-colored pieces of construction paper. Wad them up into balls and tape them to various lengths of string. Hang them around your classroom—above students' desks, above aisles, or anywhere the traffic is thickest. The more in the way they are, the better. Have your students pull them down and read them to the rest of the class.

STICK IT UP ▶ 5

Fasten a picture, word poster, or prop to the end of a yardstick or pole. Walk around the classroom with this portable teaching aid—or ask a student to do the walking. (I once stuck a yardstick down the back of my shirt and had a "brainstorming cloud" floating above my head for the entire lesson—it was very effective!) Or prepare several sticks and give them to students. Have the students line up in the front of the room and hold their sticks high in the air on cue.

FRAMED ▶ 6

Collect an assortment of picture frames; they come in a variety of sizes, shapes, and designs. Slide lesson pictures or words into each frame and place them (facing backwards) on a table in the front of the room. Turn each frame around so the students can see it as the information comes up in the lesson.

THE OTHER HALF ▶ 7

Write or draw lesson ideas on pieces of tagboard or construction paper. Cut them in half. Keep one half and hide the other (or give it to a student). Match up the halves and discuss the results as part of the lesson.

CLOTHESLINE LEARNING

This teaching technique "lays it on the line." Stretch a rope, cord, or thick piece of twine from one end of the room to the other and secure it as you would a laundry line for drying clothes. Pin up visuals with clothespins or paper clips as they are developed in the lesson. For variety, write important words or concepts on fabric or old articles of clothing instead of paper. You can even add props that relate to the lesson, such as tennis shoes (or a banana?). If you don't have a convenient place to fasten the ends of your clothesline, ask two students to hold it.

9 — STACKERS

Tape words or pictures to boxes or blocks, depending on how large you want your display to be. As your lesson progresses, stack the objects on top of one another. The higher you stack them, the more motivating and exciting it will be for your students—especially when it looks as if the whole stack may tumble down.

10 — SECRET RECIPE

Break the lesson down into parts and assign each one a "recipe" ingredient (marbles, game pieces, shells, stones, beans, and so on). Assemble the ingredients as you teach the concept or skill. At the end of the lesson, serve a portion to each student. Ask them to identify the ingredients for review. (For added interest, wear a chef's hat.)

VELCRO SUIT

Find an old suit with personality—perhaps something in polyester, like a leisure suit from the late 60's or early 70's. With a hot glue gun, fasten velcro tabs all over the jacket (and pants, for extra punch). Then stick velcro tabs to the backs of your visuals. Add the visuals to your suit as you proceed through the lesson.

CUBED CONCEPTS

Wrap a sturdy box with heavy-duty paper. (For added durability and future use, try contact paper instead.) Tape visuals to each surface. Put your cube on a stool or a table and display the appropriate surface as it comes up during the lesson. *Example:* To teach the four elements of flight, you might want to label four sides "Lift," "Thrust," "Drag," and "Gravity."

FABRIC SCRAPS

Instead of creating visuals with paper, substitute fabric scraps. Using permanent markers, write key words, questions, or phrases on scraps of varying types, sizes, and colors. (Try knits for elasticity.) Hide the scraps throughout the room—or on your person (in your pockets or socks, under your collar, in a purse, tucked into a shirt sleeve). Pull them out like handkerchiefs as you need them during the lesson.

14 ■ OBJECT LESSONS ■

HOW IS THIS LOLLIPOP LIKE OUR MAIN CHARACTER?

Analyze the content of your lesson and think of objects you might use to symbolize lesson concepts. *Examples:* A road map could represent "follow directions," a lollipop might symbolize the "sweet" qualities of a main character in a book or story. You may need to spend some time brainstorming ideas, but it's worth it—especially for the concrete visual learners in your classroom.

15 ■ STICK-ONS ■

Tape visuals to yourself, selected students, walls, windows, floor, ceiling, or anywhere else that comes to mind. The more unusual the location, the more your students will take notice. Just make sure that the visuals are placed where everyone can see them.

16 ■ RAISE IT UP ■

Rig up a simple pulley system from the ceiling. (Get a pulley from the hardware store or create your own with string and a wire circle made from a coat hanger—whatever works!) Attach a visual or prop to the end of the string signifying the lesson theme or objective. As the lesson develops, pull the visual or prop off the ground with the string, eventually lifting it to the ceiling by the lesson's end. *Tip:* Rather than holding the string for the whole lesson, secure the end to a table or chair leg each time you move it, or ask a student to hold it for you.

PLAY BALL

Tape lesson information to *soft* balls (Nerf balls, sponge balls, inflatable beach balls, or lightweight plastic balls found in grocery and toy stores). Toss them to students and have them read the information. Have them throw the balls back to you so you can attach additional lesson material and start the process over again. Repeat until the lesson is finished. *Tip:* Save time by taping envelopes to the balls and placing lesson information inside the envelopes.

MAGIC CARPET

Find a rug your students can sit around (or on, if it's big enough) as you present your lesson. Or adopt another gimmick that becomes synonymous with your teaching, such as a special hat or vest. Try using different ones to represent different subjects—a Math Hat, a Social Studies Scarf, or a Reading Jacket. Put it on to signal the start of a lesson.

SCRIBBLE SKETCHES

Using paper, the chalkboard, or an overhead transparency, scribble-sketch lesson scenes or ideas. Your art work doesn't have to be perfect or beautiful; it simply has to communicate. The example shows a scribble-sketch from a social studies lesson on the Westward Movement.

CONESTOGA WAGON

20 ▸ GET THE POINT

Use a pointer to emphasize and clarify lesson ideas. You don't need to have an "official" pointer. Anything long and thin will do: a yardstick, cane, TV antenna, stick from a tree—whatever works. Use it often and your students will associate you with it. You may want to sign your name to it or decorate it in a novel way (bright paint, colored tape, ribbons, glitter).

21 ▸ PICTURE PUZZLE

Any visual consisting of words and/or pictures can be cut up into a puzzle of about 5 to 10 pieces, or any quantity that corresponds to the number of ideas you are trying to get across in a lesson. As you proceed through the lesson, add and assemble the puzzle pieces. Talk about the significance of each piece as you add it to the puzzle.

22 ▸ FELT FRIENDS

Using permanent markers, draw or write lesson materials on pieces of felt. Look for students who are wearing clothing made of wool or cotton. (Felt won't stick to smooth or silky surfaces.) Place these "felt friends" on your students and teach away!

GIANT CARDS

Cut a piece of tagboard in half and decorate one half with a large question mark. On the other half, write or tape lesson information. Rest the cards on a chalk tray or mount them on a wall. Turn them around to share the lesson material as it comes up during instruction. For durability, laminate the cards or cover them with contact paper and write on them with dry-erase markers.

WEATHER WORKS

Center lesson themes around current weather conditions or seasons. *Suggestions:* For fall: Write ideas/questions on leaves. For winter: Build a miniature snowman, a piece at a time, as you "build" a lesson. For spring: Pull petals off a flower as you introduce new ideas or concepts. For summer: Pin words and visuals to colorful beach towels.

THE SANDBOX

Trim a cardboard box down to the height of 4" or find an old cake pan. Fill it with sand. Create words, characters, scenery, and props out of pieces of tagboard and tape them to popsicle sticks or pencils. (Draw your own pictures or cut pictures out of magazines.) Poke the sticks into the sand, then move and manipulate them as you present the lesson. A sandbox is a wonderful tool for dramatizing an episode from history, a chapter from a book, or a student story. *Tip:* For scenery ideas, see Fascinating Backgrounds, pages 87–116.

FLEXIBLE MOBILE

Make a generic mobile that can be used over and over again. Construct the frame out of wood strips or coathanger wire. Fasten string or fishing line to strategic points of balance. Attach a paper clip to the end of each string. Now you can suspend pieces of paper or other lightweight objects from different points on your mobile. *Variation:* Hang words or props from a dead branch potted in a plant stand.

ADD

SUBTRACT

MULTIPLY

DIVIDE

CRUMPLED

Students are used to seeing lesson materials neat, clean, and wrinkle-free. Surprise your class by crumpling up lesson visuals into paper balls. Suspend them from strings attached to the ceiling, balance them on pop bottles, or toss them into the room like baseballs. Add interest with colored construction paper.

BOTTOMS UP

Select two or more students to sit on a sturdy table with their legs dangling loosely over the edge. Tape words, faces of characters, etc. to the bottoms of their shoes. Have them lift their feet as appropriate during the lesson. You might work out a system of "signals," such as raising your right hand (or eyebrow) when you want a student to raise his or her right foot. If each shoe bottom is a different character in a story, students should lift their feet when they hear their character's name.

SOGGY LESSONS

Write messages on paper or fabric with permanent markers. Put them in a large glass bowl and fill the bowl with water. (The *last* one you will need should go into the bowl *first* so the *first* one you need is on top.) As you move through the lesson, pull the messages out of the bowl, ring them out, and share them with the class. If you think you might want to re-use them, hang them up to drip-dry on a makeshift laundry line.

IT ALL ADDS UP

Find an old wooden stool or chair. Use a permanent marker to label it with key words or phrases from a particular subject area, one at a time. This works whether you are teaching a concept (such as respect) or a skill (such as double-digit division). As you record each day's word or phrase, students will see the continuity of the lessons and begin to understand that it all adds up.

ON A ROLL

Write lesson objectives, questions, statements, or concepts with marker on adding machine tape. Use BIG letters. Roll out the tape on the floor as if you are rolling out a carpet. Ask student assistants to hold up the tape, which will stretch from one end of the room to the other (or perhaps all around the room). Read it aloud together as a class.

32 ━━━━ TV TEACHER ━━━━

Construct a cardboard TV set from a box, wire, aluminum foil, plastic knobs, pieces of screen—anything you can find. Cut out the bottom and the screen area and wear it on your head.

33 ━━━━ FACE PAINTING ━━━━

Ask for a student volunteer who doesn't mind getting a little dirty. Using tempera paint or face paints, quickly decorate his or her face to tie into an aspect of the lesson. *Examples:* if you're teaching about animals, paint the student's face with whiskers, stripes, or other appropriate characteristics. If you're teaching about emotions, you might paint the student's face blue (sadness), red (anger/embarrassment), or green (jealousy/envy).

34 ━━━━ RIPPING REVIEW ━━━━

Write or draw quick visuals to be used for a lesson. Don't spend a lot of time on them, because as you finish talking about each one, you'll tear it in half. Conclude the lesson by piecing the halves together for review, or ask for student volunteers.

35 ━━━━ AIR MAIL ━━━━

Write lesson information or messages on pieces of paper, fold them into paper airplanes, and sail them into your classroom. The student who catches each paper airplane should open it up and read it to the class.

TURN THE TABLES

Tape newsprint to the top of a card table or other small table. Turn the table on its side. Use it as an instructional tool, just as you would the chalkboard or overhead projector. This makes a handy portable writing surface for anyplace that doesn't have one, such as the corner of a room. (I use mine for small-group discussions.)

THE TEACHING TIE

You may use a regular tie, but it's more fun with an outrageous or even ugly tie. Tape words or other visuals to it, then move around the room. As you refer to key lesson points, your students' eyes will be on you. *Tip:* Ties aren't just for men, but women who aren't comfortable wearing them can try a scarf instead.

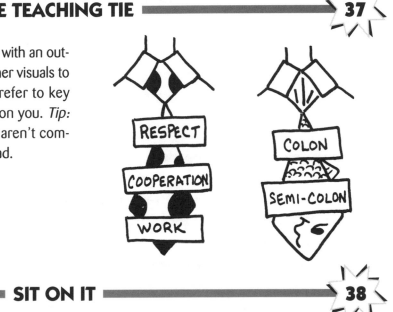

SIT ON IT

Set up a row of chairs in front of the room. Fasten key words or visuals to the back of each chair. Select students to sit in the chairs and face the class. Whenever you introduce a lesson idea that is taped to the back of a chair, instruct the student to turn the chair around, exposing the idea to the class.

When you are reviewing material for a test or have something else you want your students to remember, develop a special cue to remind them that what you are about to say is very important. You might say, "When I put my finger on my nose, this means that you should listen carefully to what I say next, because you will definitely see it on a test." Or "When I put this hat on, please write down what I say, because it is something you really need to know." *Tip:* Use this technique sparingly or it will lose its effectiveness. For example, you should wear a special hat only during key points of the lesson, not for the whole class period.

40 THE ART OF WRITING

Writing on the board, paper, or overhead can become routine and boring. At times, try varying your writing style with a creative twist. There are many ways to turn written communication into artistic expression. *Suggestions:*

▶ Vary the size and shape of letters.

▶ Draw words in ways that reflect their meaning. The letters in "up" might be tall and thin. The letters in "tired" might be bent-over or droopy. The e's in "see" could be a pair of eyes. Surround "surprise" with exclamation points.

▶ Write in circles, slants, curves, or angles—anything but straight lines.

▶ Use colored chalk or markers.

▶ Use balloon letters (see page 85).

STORY APRON

41

A kitchen apron or carpenter's apron can serve as a portable lesson display. As you teach, move around the room and tape or pin visuals to it. The more pockets, the better, since they make excellent storage compartments.

PERSONIFICATION

42

Find objects that relate to the lesson, whether directly or indirectly. Give them human qualities by attaching eyes, ears, nose, mouth, and hair. *Example:* If you are teaching the poem "Casey at the Bat," bring a baseball bat to life by attaching paper eyes and a mouth and yarn hair. (For drawing tips and ideas, see A Basic Course in Cartooning, pages 57–85.)

ANYTHING GOES

43

This technique brings all of your natural creativity, spontaneity, and intuition into play. As you are teaching, reach for anything that symbolizes some aspect of the lesson. *Examples:* If you are teaching "The Three Little Pigs," build a brick house out of books. Call on students to act out a word problem in math. Think of everything in your classroom—and every*one* in it—as a potential teaching tool.

Pre-assemble a "sculpture" that relates to the lesson—or build it in front of the class. This might be a character or a concept. Use tape, glue, play dough, chewing gum—whatever it takes to make your creation. Build it on a table or a cardboard base, or dangle it on a heavy string from the ceiling. If you assemble your sculpture "live" in front of your class, talk about each item as you attach it. *Variation:* Collect props, visuals, or other items that relate to a unit of study. Tie, tape, or glue them together, one or two pieces at a time, over the course of the unit. When it is finished, set it on a table or dangle it from the ceiling. Students should be able to identify each object and recognize its significance to the unit. It might look like a "blob," but it's really a unit review!

Another variation on the junk sculpture. This time, build a character out of boxes, pop bottles, cans, yarn, cardboard tubes, fabric, and anything else you can think of. Give your character a name (or ask your students for suggestions). Refer to it at various points during the lesson or all through the unit. You might say, "Today Ms. Tinhead is going to teach us about eclipses," or "Mr. Broombody will guide us through the digestive system this afternoon."

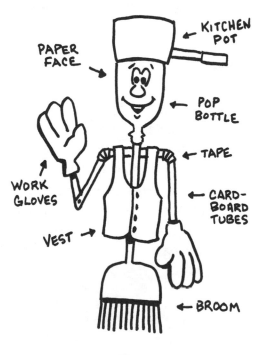

STUFFED

Wear loose-fitting clothes (sweats are best) and stuff lesson props all over—in your shirt, pants, sleeves, pockets, socks, shoes. Pull them out as needed for instruction. *Example:* For a lesson on personal hygiene, you might stuff these items under your clothes: toothpaste tube, toothbrush, dental floss, soap, shampoo, wash cloth, deodorant, towel. (The key is to *remember* where you put things so you can pull out the right item at the right time.) Occasionally you might want to tease your class by letting part of an object (such as a hairbrush handle) stick out for them to see and guess about.

GONE FISHIN'

Attach a clothespin or paper clip to the end of a fishing pole line. (Your fishing pole can be a stick with a string attached to it—nothing fancy.) Write lesson material on note cards or collect props that relate to the lesson. Put your lesson material behind a curtain (a draped blanket works fine). Have students stick the fishing pole over the curtain. While they are fishin', attach lesson material to the line with the clothespin or paper clip. Give a little tug on the line to indicate they have caught a fish. When they lift the line out of the "water," read the information or talk about the prop. (To make your job easier, number the lesson materials and assign a student to work the "pond.") *Tip:* Create an assortment of fish out of tagboard or heavy construction paper. Laminate them and write lesson information on them with dry-erase markers. You'll use this teaching tool many times.

SCULPT & MOLD

Think of characters, concepts, or ideas that would be fairly easy to shape out of wire, tin foil, clay, play dough, or paper. Prepare them in advance or create them during the lesson (invite your students to help). *Examples:* A pink play dough heart to introduce a unit on circulation. A paper airplane to help explain the concepts of lift, thrust, drag, and gravity. Tin-foil animals to teach Kipling's *Just So Stories.*

★49★ FLOORS & CEILINGS

Floors and ceilings can be terrific teaching tools. Tape visuals, words, or props to them. Clear a space on the floor and use the area as if it were a giant chalkboard. Spread out visuals, props, and models, then walk your way through the lesson, addressing points of interest. Tape shapes to the floor. In my classroom, I use tape to create a giant replica of a human heart. My students walk through it as if they were blood cells flowing through the circulatory system, calling out each part as they travel through it. Sometimes I tape out a big boat and have my students sit in it while I teach a lesson about marine life. *Variation:* Take your lesson outdoors and use colored chalk to create shapes and outlines on the blacktop or cement pavement.

★50★ WHITEBOARDS

Write or draw on them using colored chalk or water soluble markers. Tape things to them. A whiteboard can be a versatile and creative medium for expression–yours and your students'.

★51★ FLANNEL BOARDS

Flannel boards are always fun and easy to use. Cut a piece out of an old flannel sheet or shirt and tape it around a large square or rectangle of cardboard or tagboard. Cut visuals out of felt and write on them with permanent markers. You can also use paper backed with glitter or sandpaper.

★52★ BULLETIN BOARDS

Bulletin boards add warmth, color, and personality to a classroom. They are also excellent teaching tools. You can use them to display a unit theme, outline skills, give a panoramic view of a topic, or teach a specific lesson. Mount student work on bulletin boards, use them as learning centers, or post special announcements and upcoming events. Their versatility is unlimited. If you don't have a bulletin board in your classroom, create one (or more) by gluing cork squares to a board.

SPECIAL EFFECTS

Inventive ways to stimulate the senses

Who says that we always have to teach with the lights on? Grab your students' attention by presenting a lesson in the dark. Turn out the lights, draw the blinds, or cover the windows with paper to make the room as dark as possible. Shine a high-powered flashlight on strategically-placed visuals as they come up in the lesson. For best results, mount your visuals on the walls before the students enter the room. *Variation:* Have students bring their own flashlights to class so they can see to take notes. *Tip:* Do a test-run first to make sure this works in your room.

Check out a book of magic tricks from your nearest library or media center. Learn a trick or two (they are easier than you may think). Use them from time to time to introduce lesson concepts. *Examples:* Instead of pulling a rabbit out of a hat, pull out a prop linked to your lesson. Or do a card trick with lesson words taped to the cards.

55 ━━ SHRINK & MAGNIFY ━━

If the photocopy machine at your school can reduce materials, try this technique to get your students' attention. Reduce lesson messages to the point that you can barely read them with the naked eye. Allow students to use a magnifying glass to decipher the messages. Have them read the messages aloud to the class.

56 ━━ LET IT GLOW ━━

See if your school building or district has a black light you can borrow. Using fluorescent art chalk, write lesson information on the chalkboard or black paper. Turn the lights off and do your thing. Students will be amazed at how each word jumps out as it glows in the dark.

57 ━━ FLUORESCENT MARKERS, PAINTS & CHALK ━━

The next best thing to a black light is simply to use fluorescent markers, paint, or chalk under normal lighting conditions. (Be sure to get the chalk designed for art projects, not the kind for chalkboards. Ask the art teacher at your school or check with your local art supplies store.) For white or light-colored surfaces, use translucent colors. Opaque colors on a black surface (try construction paper) come the closest to creating a black light effect, even with the lights on.

Create a simple "secret code." (I recommend an alphabet code—basic graphic symbols for all 26 letters of the alphabet.) Select key words or concepts in the lesson and write them in code on the board. Mount a large "code key" on a wall in your classroom so you can use this technique several times during the year.

VOWEL VULTURE ═══➤ 59

Write lesson words and phrases using consonants only—no vowels. Tell your students that the "vowel vulture" has gobbled up the vowels. It's surprisingly easy to read vowel-less words.

SILENCE IS GOLDEN ═══➤ 60

Some lessons or activities require little verbal direction. Try "directing" your students without saying a word. Make up a story about how you have lost your voice. Or pretend that you can talk only when you are standing in a certain area of the room or holding a particular object in your hand (such as a "magic" roll of paper towel); it's nice to have the option of talking if you need to explain or clarify something with the group or an individual. Otherwise, teach with body language, written words, pictures, and so on.

BELLS, BEEPS & BONGS

Use this technique when your students are working independently or in cooperative groups. As you change points of interest or lesson topics, or when you simply want the attention of the class, ring a bell, beep a bicycle horn, bong a cake pan with a spoon, ding a triangle—anything you choose. Explain in advance that when students hear this sound, they must turn to you, then *freeze* from head to foot. No moving or talking allowed! All eyes and ears should be on you because what you are about to say is very important. *Variations:* Relate the sound to the lesson. You might play a bar or two of ethnic music, a few words from a speech, or an appropriate sound effect (jet plane flying overhead, dogs barking, birds singing). Check your local library or media center for tapes or CDs of sound effects and cue up the sound you want ahead of time.

ALL TOGETHER NOW

Make a transparency of page 27. As you present your lesson, periodically have your students chant in unison the words or phrases you point to on the chart. (If my words don't fit your purposes, feel free to make your own chart.) *Examples:* When you say something very important that you want your students to remember, point to "COULD YOU REPEAT THAT PLEASE?" After the class chants the phrase, you might respond, "I WOULD LOVE TO!" If you feel that the lesson is losing steam, you have belabored a point, or it's time to move on, point to "LET'S MOVE ON NOW." You might respond, "GOOD IDEA!"

SUPER

TERRIFIC

WHAT DID YOU SAY?

WOW

OUTRAGEOUS

GOOD IDEA

INCREDIBLE

YES

I AGREE

I NEVER THOUGHT OF THAT BEFORE

NO

YOU DON'T SAY

TRUE

ABSOLUTELY

I DON'T AGREE

I WOULD LOVE TO

YEE-HA!

THANKS

OOOo

ARE YOU SURE?

I LIKE IT

IT'S SO SIMPLE

LET'S MOVE ON NOW

FALSE

GIVE ME A BREAK

I UNDERSTAND

COULD YOU REPEAT THAT PLEASE?

64 ▪ WHO SAID THAT? ▪

DUCK VOICE!

Can you do impersonations or change your voice in other ways? (Can you talk like a duck?) Share your talent with your students. Use a special cue to let your class know that you're about to change into someone (or something) else; you might put on a special hat or jacket, take a drink from a special cup, or go to a different part of the room. Then let your voice mysteriously change. Or use a variety of voices to match different parts of the lesson. Get into character and grab your students' attention.

65 ▪ PUSHING BUTTONS ▪

I learned this technique from David Pendleton, a nationally known ventriloquist. He put his finger at the back of a volunteer's neck and told him to open his mouth each time David pushed an imaginary button on his neck. David then told his story through his human "dummy." As a teacher, you can use the same technique as you share key points of interest from your lesson. Don't worry about whether your mouth moves; cover it up with a book, handkerchief, or piece of paper.

66 ▪ ECHO ▪

Some words from your lesson are worth repeating. Why should you have to say them twice? Select a student to be your "echo." When you tap the student on the head, he or she will repeat whatever you just said. Keep your thoughts brief and to the point. Break them up into phrases so it's easy for students to recite them.

CONTAINERS, COMPARTMENTS & COVER-UPS

**Learning "packages" that promote
curiosity, anticipation, and motivation**

BE A CONTAINER COLLECTOR 67

Collect an assortment of containers that can be stored and accessed easily. Cereal boxes, food boxes, decorative boxes and bags all fold up flat for easy storage. Wood, tin, and plastic containers of varying sizes are durable and stackable. Gather fabric remnants, blankets, and scarves to lay over lesson materials as cover-ups. Where can you find these valuable tools of the teaching trade? Check your family storage areas; comb garage sales or tag sales. Then set up an organizational system for your collection.

THE SUITCASE 68

Buy, find, or borrow a special suitcase (or backpack, sack, or tote bag) that will become your traveling trademark. I came across an old leather suitcase that had belonged to my wife's grandmother; it has a lot of class and personality. Pack your bag with props, papers, and other items you will need for the lesson, and pull them out as you need them. Your students will look forward to seeing what's in your suitcase.

69 — BALLOON BUST

Write lesson messages on small pieces of paper and stuff them into balloons. Then blow up and tie the balloons. Pop each balloon as the messages are needed for instruction, and read them to the class. (Check first to see that none of your students are afraid of popping balloons; some people are.)

70 — UNDERCOVER

Instead of exposing a variety of props and lesson materials to your students all at once, cover them up with an attractive blanket or piece of cloth. Uncover each item as needed during the lesson. This simple technique will keep students focused by making them wonder what is still "undercover."

71 — DON'T LOOK DOWN

While the students are out of the room, tape lesson messages under their chairs, desks, or tables. Instruct individual students to look under their chairs, desks, or tables when specifically asked to do so. Have them share their messages with the class.

THE ENVELOPE, PLEASE

Make jumbo envelopes out of two pieces of tagboard stapled or taped together. Laminate the pieces ahead of time for durability and future use. Pull information out of the envelopes as you present the lesson. *Tip:* Use large envelopes for information you want the whole class to see, regular envelopes or folders for individuals or small groups.

HIDE-AND-SEEK

Hide lesson materials around the room—drawings, pictures, worksheets, props—in strategic and unexpected locations. Select one or more students to find the materials. Encourage them by playing "Hot and Cold." As they are moving around the room trying to find the items, encourage them by saying "warm...hot...hotter...BOILING!" as they get closer to an object. If they move away from it, say "cold...colder...FREEZING!" Read or display the materials when they are found.

THE BELL JAR

Place lesson props and visuals inside large glass jars or bowls (string and tape works fine) and turn them upside down. The students can see the dangling objects but can't touch them.

I have tried this with my students and it works very well, provided you do some advance planning. Start by choosing a student who is a good sport and can take a little teasing. Talk to the student privately and explain what you will be doing. (You will need to arrange to talk without calling other students' attention to the fact, or the joke won't work.) Then, while all of the students are out of the room, hide an important item from your lesson (for example, a packet of worksheets) in that student's desk, book, folder, or wherever. As the class enters the room, put on a show of looking everywhere for the missing item. Explain that you can't start the lesson until you find what you are looking for. Ask the students if they have seen the item. Finally, out of desperation, ask the class to open their desks (books, folders) to be searched. Pretend that you are earnestly looking and meander toward your student co-conspirator. "Find" the missing item and, in a *joking* manner, begin to question the student. Eventually the rest of the class will realize what's going on (especially if you and the student start laughing together). If not, make sure that they do understand. Meanwhile, your classroom "drama" will have drawn everyone's attention.

WATERTIGHT

Put lesson messages or props in watertight containers such as plastic bags or 35mm film containers. Label them in the order you will need them for the lesson (A, B, C..., 1, 2, 3...) and place them in a pail of water. Call on individual students to pull the containers out of the water, open them, and share their contents with the class.

LITTLE BROWN BAG

Use a brown paper lunch bag to unleash your students' imaginations. As you present the lesson verbally, pull *imaginary* props out of the bag. These can be anything you choose, of any size you please—blocks, a microscope, a locomotive, *Tyrannosaurus rex.* Use your mime skills and add sound effects. Your students will be fascinated by the "contents" of your little brown bag.

THE LITTLE BROWN BAG

MEMOS & MESSAGES

MELISSA

Everyone enjoys getting messages. Make a special pocket folder for each student out of file folders, envelopes, or construction paper. Laminate them and mount them on walls or sides of desks. Then write notes to your students and tuck them into their pocket folders. Your notes might be anything related to the lesson—questions, the session objectives, key words or phrases. Call on students to read their notes aloud to the class.

OVERHEAD, SLIDE & OPAQUE PROJECTORS

New uses for tried-and-true classroom tools

The overhead projector has four distinct advantages in the classroom:

▶ It works equally well for both large- and small-group instruction.

▶ You can maintain eye contact with your students. You don't have to turn your back on them, as you do when you're using the chalkboard.

▶ Lights only need to be dimmed—the room doesn't need to be totally dark—so your students can still take notes.

▶ It's a great time-saver. Once you make a set of transparencies, you can save them, file them, and use them over and over again. Transparencies are terrific for emphasis or review.

8 WAYS TO MAKE THE MOST OF YOUR OVERHEAD PROJECTOR

1. Set the projector on a low cart so you don't obstruct your students' view.

2. If possible, prepare your transparencies ahead of time instead of writing information on them while the lesson is in progress.

3. Keep your transparencies simple. Spread out your text and graphics over the whole surface area. Overcrowding information makes it confusing and hard to follow. Use a series of transparencies rather than packing too much material into one.

4. Use lined paper or graph paper as a guide to help you write in straight lines. Just place it behind the transparency while preparing it.

5. Use plain paper to cover up sections of the transparency you don't yet want your students to see. This helps your students to focus on specific areas.

6. Use a thin pencil or pen as a pointer. Lay it directly on the transparency to indicate areas of interest during the lesson.

7. Add color and punch to your transparencies with permanent or water-soluble markers.

8. Use the photocopy machine to make professional-looking transparencies. Anything drawn or printed on regular paper can be copied onto a transparency. *Examples:* student worksheets, charts, illustrations, text.

79 FLIPS & OVERLAYS

For emphasis, flip a word or phrase (written on piece of transparency material) onto a blank section of the transparency. Or overlay a piece of opaque paper onto the transparency to cover up a word or phrase, then lift it to uncover your message. Cardboard transparency frames, available at office supply stores, are good bases for securing flips and overlays with tape.

80 ILLUSTRATIONS

Instead of writing words on a transparency, try drawing. Doodles, pictures, and symbols can convey your message just as effectively. Illustrations work especially well for stories. They don't have to be fancy to communicate; don't worry if you "can't draw." Check out the Basic Course in Cartooning on pages 57–85 for ideas.

81 BLACKOUT

Cut out paper silhouettes of objects representing lesson components. When you place them on the overhead projector, they will case opaque shadows on the screen. *Examples:* Use silhouettes of a boy, dog, tree, sun, and grass (as shown) if you're telling a story about them. Or assemble pieces of a pie as you explain fractions. Cutouts can be manipulated to dramatize different aspects of the lesson. They are a simple and effective way to animate a text. Store them in envelopes for future use.

OPAQUE & TRANSPARENT TOGETHER 82

Combine transparent visuals with opaque cut-outs for an interesting effect. In the example, the boat is drawn on the transparency, while the water is an opaque cut-out placed on the projector. If you're telling a story about a sinking ship, it's easy to make the water rise and rise.... *Tip:* See Fascinating Backgrounds on pages 87–116 for all kinds of possibilities; simply photocopy them onto transparencies.

THE SHADOWBOX 83

Construct a large wooden frame and attach a white bedsheet with tacks, as shown in the illustration. Place the overhead projector behind the screen and position paper cut-outs of lesson ideas on the projector. Shadowbox images will come to life on the screen. This is a wonderful technique for storytelling; one person can narrate the story while another manipulates cut-out patterns projected onto the screen. Store cutouts in envelopes for future use.

84 ═══ WALLPAPER ═══

Project an overhead transparency onto a large piece of blank newsprint or butcher paper rather than the usual movie screen. Surprise your students by writing right on the paper. *Example:* Put a transparency of the heart and its chambers on the overhead projector. Project it onto the paper and use a red marker to trace the flow of blood through the heart.

85 ═══ STUDENT TEACHING ═══

Students love to prepare work for display on the overhead. Give each student a topic, a blank transparency, markers, and a little time. They will create powerful visuals you can use in your lesson...and you won't have to do a thing.

86 ═══ MAKING CORRECTIONS ═══

The overhead projector is an ideal teaching and correcting tool. Simply make a transparency of the activity sheet or test and project it onto the screen. (Depending on the nature of the activity or test, you can even have your students write their answers on lined paper—you don't need to make a copy for every student.) Fill in the answers during corrections for all to see.

87 ═══ BIGGER IS BETTER ═══

When you need to enlarge lesson material for display, the overhead is an excellent alternative to the opaque projector. Make a transparency of the material and project it onto paper, cardboard, or tagboard. Trace the words or images with black permanent marker. If you want to add color, remove your tracing from the wall and color it with markers or paints.

SUPER SLIDES ➤ 88

Slides are far more versatile than regular picture prints because they can be shown to large groups. Take pictures of things that relate to your lessons—types of buildings if you're teaching about architecture, wildlife for ecology. Give upper elementary students power over this medium by letting them shoot slides for classroom projects.

CREATE YOUR OWN SLIDES ➤ 89

Blank slides, available at professional camera supply stores, can be written on or drawn on with extra-fine, felt-tipped permanent markers. You and your students can create your own slides without the expense of film developing, and they have many possible uses. *Examples:* Headings, titles, and credits for a presentation; to illustrate a song or a story.

THE PROFESSIONAL TOUCH ➤ 90

Add a professional touch to classroom slide shows with background music, sound effects, and narration. Putting your slides in the order you want and playing music to match the mood is a simple way to enhance your presentation. Check with your school AV or media department to find out about other technologies available to you; it's possible to get quite sophisticated if you know what you're doing.

HUMAN SLIDES

Here's a fun and creative alternative to taking pictures and developing them: Have students pose for life-size "slides" during the lesson! First, come up with a series of "still-shot frame" ideas. *Examples:* Scenes from a story; historical events (Washington crossing the Delaware?); vocabulary words (acted out in a sequence of slides). Next, select students (or ask for volunteers) to role play the slides. Set up a slide projector in the front of the room. Have two students hold up a curtain (a bed sheet works fine) to conceal between-slide changes. Push the slide projector button to signal the curtain-holders to drop the curtain showing the human slide, then proceed with your narration. *Tips:* Allow time for students to rehearse their slide poses. Behind your makeshift stage area, tape a list of scenes so your actors know the sequence of events. Keep props to a minimum and let students use their imaginations. Set a no-talking-behind-the-curtain rule, since conversation (and laughter) will distract your audience. Finally: As students are changing scenes, keep your audience interested by playing background music, continuing your narration, or having mini-discussions. *Variations:* Slide shows usually include a few funny "mistakes"—slides that are in backwards or upside-down. You might include one or two for extra entertainment. Have the students in a scene face away from the class, say "Oops— that slide is in the wrong way!", then raise the curtain and have them quickly shift to facing forward before lowering the curtain again. Or have a student stand on his or her head to indicate an upside-down slide.

HUMAN SLIDE POSE

CURTAIN CREW MEMBER

CURTAIN CREW MEMBER

CURTAIN

INSTANT POSTERS

The opaque projector enlarges prints or images and projects them onto a wall or screen. This handy tool is rarely used for instructional purposes, and there are many ways you can capitalize on its unique features. One of the best and most versatile is to place illustrations on the machine and project them onto paper or tagboard. Outline with black marker and color with tempera paints, watercolors, or colored permanent markers. You'll create high-quality posters and displays with minimum effort.

LARGE-GROUP VISUALS

Use the opaque projector to enlarge all kinds of visuals for the whole class to see. Students might show special pictures or flat projects (collages, charts, displays). When you read stories with pictures to your class, put the pictures under the opaque machine–this is far more effective than showing the small prints in the book. As you come across pictures, quotations, graphs, etc. that reinforce lesson elements, utilize the power of the opaque projector to share them with your class.

OPAQUE FILMSTRIPS

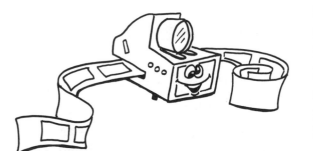

To change visuals on an opaque projector, you must lower the display tray, remove the current visual, put the next one on, and slide the tray back into place. This technique eliminates that time-consuming process. Simply tape your visuals together to make a continuous roll, then pull each one into the projection area as needed. Save your "opaque filmstrips" for future lessons or reviews.

MOVIES, FILMSTRIPS & VIDEOS

Creative ways to open your students' eyes

Movies, filmstrips, and videos are powerful teaching tools when used with planning, purpose, and imagination. For best results, always remember this cardinal rule: *Thou shalt always tell your students what to look for and attach some relevance to their life.*

In other words, it's not enough to flip the "on" switch and stay out of the way. You must give your students specific instructions about what to watch for and why, making the experience personally meaningful for them. They need a "target" to guide their thinking, and they need to have a reason to pay attention. This is the way to stimulate learning and retention. They also need to be held accountable for what they see.

On the following page, you'll find a generic activity sheet that can be used with any movie, filmstrip, or video. Make several copies and have them available to hand out before you dim the lights. Following are some suggestions for "target topics." Direct your students to watch for one or more, or develop your own list of "target topics."

- ▶ The "Big Idea"
- ▶ Fascinating facts
- ▶ How-to steps
- ▶ What if...?
- ▶ Key words (identify these for your students, or have them identify key words)
- ▶ The links in a chain of events

- ▶ Facts about the main character's life, achievements, problems
- ▶ Feelings evoked while watching
- ▶ Main principles presented
- ▶ Personal meaning/relevance (ask "What does this movie/filmstrip/video mean to you? How can you apply it to your life?")

Notice that the activity sheet also provides a place for students to rate what they have just seen. These ratings will help you decide which movies, filmstrips, and videos are worth repeating in future classes.

MEDIA "MINUTES"

NAME(S): _____

TITLE: _____ DATE: _____

TASK TO ACCOMPLISH: _____

_____

_____

NOTES: _____

_____

_____

_____

_____

_____

_____

_____

_____

_____

_____

_____

_____

RATING: 1   2   3   4   5   ⟨CIRCLE⟩
          LOW   HIGH

EXPECT THE UNEXPECTED

Where is it written that we have to show films on a movie screen? Try projecting onto a white wall, blank newsprint paper taped to the wall, or even the ceiling. To emphasize key points, show different parts of the film on different walls (or a walls-and-ceiling combination).

PARTS & PORTIONS

Who says we have to show a movie from beginning to end? Skip a section and ask your students to imagine or predict what happened in the part they didn't see. This technique works especially well with stories. Perhaps the simplest and most satisfying variation is to show everything but the ending, have the students predict it, then show it afterward and discuss how close their predictions came.

CREATIVE COMBINATIONS

While you're showing a film or video, put transparencies of key concepts or questions on the overhead projector. Or hold up a prop related to an idea presented in a filmstrip. This technique requires some advance planning, but it can make a movie, filmstrip, or video twice as interesting.

STOP & REPEAT

You don't have to wait until the end of a film to hold a discussion or a question-and-answer session. Stop and start it whenever you want to emphasize a point or explain an idea. Rewind a segment and show it again if it's especially interesting or important—or if it moves too quickly for some of your students to grasp.

TEAM EFFORTS

Have students work in pairs or small groups to watch for "target topics," themes, or important information. Afterward, have them share their information with the class. *Example:* If you're showing a video about weather, you might have one group watch for how clouds are formed, another report on the different cloud formations, a third pay attention to information on the types of moisture, and a fourth look at how barometric pressure affects the weather. As the groups share their information, everyone reaps the benefits of a thorough review.

GOOD QUESTIONS

Instruct your students to write 5-10 questions about the movie, filmstrip, or video while they are watching it. Use their questions for discussions, quizzes, or tests. If necessary, guide them in formulating good questions. They should emphasize general concepts, processes, or skills instead of trivia that few students will remember or need to know. *Examples of good questions:* "Who wrote the Declaration of Independence?" "Why was the Declaration of Independence important?" *Examples of poor questions:* "What time of day was the Declaration of Independence written?" "What kind of paper was the Declaration of Independence written on?"

THE LEARNING CENTER

If possible, set up a learning center in a corner of your classroom. You'll need basic equipment (cassette player, TV and VCR, 16mm projector, filmstrip projector, screen or white wall, headphone sets, etc.) and a junction box (check with your school AV or media department). Once your learning center is established, divide your class into small groups of 6 to 10 students each. Rotate the groups through the learning center. It will quickly become a favorite place in your classroom—a quiet place for independent learning that requires minimal teacher supervision. Be sure to set some ground rules in advance.

103 ## STILL SHOTS, SLO-MO & REVERSE ACTION

Slow down or stop any 16mm film to emphasize key points. (Some VCRs also let you do this with videos.) This technique is especially useful for showing motion (an athlete running, salmon swimming upstream) or focusing in on specific events in science and nature films. Or break from routine and show an action scene in reverse—a science experiment, a sports event, a chase. This is an instant attention-grabber.

104 ## CRITIC'S CHOICE

After viewing a movie, filmstrip, or video, have your students rate it as if they were film critics. Ask them to tell what they liked and didn't like and to share any other thoughts and ideas. Come up with a class rating. (If you use the Media Minutes activity sheet, you can collect the ratings and average them to obtain a class rating.)

Blank filmstrips are available at camera stores for a nominal fee. Use fine-tipped markers to create your own filmstrips, or have students make filmstrips for special projects or reports. It's fun and the results can be incredible. On the following pages, you'll find two activity sheets that may be used for planning filmstrips before transferring them to blanks. Make several copies to have available whenever the need arises. *Tip:* Check a commercial filmstrip to find out the size of each frame. (Count the sprocket holes along the sides.) Then draw lines to separate the frames before starting your filmstrips. Otherwise the images may be too large or too small to project correctly.

Often a filmstrip has excellent pictures, but the narration is outdated, inappropriate for a particular age group, or boring. Why not write your own script? Bring to light what you feel is most important to the lesson.

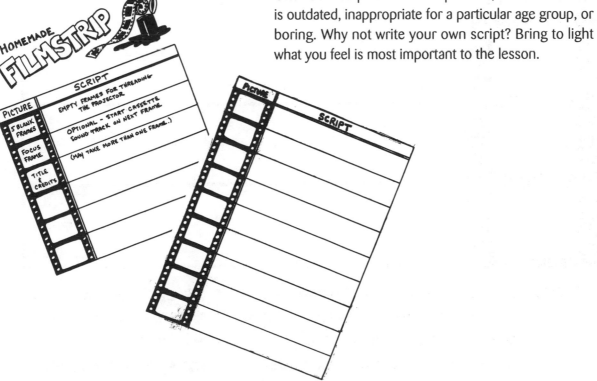

HOMEMADE FILMSTRIP

PICTURE	SCRIPT
5 BLANK FRAMES	EMPTY FRAMES FOR THREADING THE PROJECTOR
FOCUS FRAME	OPTIONAL – START CASSETTE SOUND TRACK ON NEXT FRAME
TITLE & CREDITS	(MAY TAKE MORE THAN ONE FRAME.)

TIPS:
- USE ULTRA-FINE PERMANENT FELT-TIPPED MARKERS
- USE FINGERNAIL POLISH REMOVER TO ERASE MISTAKES
- KEEP DRAWINGS SIMPLE, USE ACTION, VARY PICTURES
- USE BACKGROUND MUSIC, SOUND EFFECTS, & A SOOTHING BEEP OR BELL TONE BETWEEN SLIDES
- VARY VOICE TONE AND VOCAL EXPRESSION

PICTURE	SCRIPT

VIDEO TIPS

The video camera is an easy-to-use, powerfully effective motivational and educational tool, once you master a few basics. Following are 7 production tips to help you make the most of your video camera.

1. ***The how-to's of taping.*** If you are not familiar with the camera, read the owner's manual or get instruction from someone who is familiar with it (ask at your school AV department—or in your classroom; you may find an expert among your students). Most video cameras today are extremely simple to operate: just turn the power button on, look through the viewfinder at whatever you want to tape, push the red button to start recording, and push it again to stop recording.

2. ***Power source.*** If you are using the battery pack rather than an electrical outlet as your main power source, make sure that it's fully charged the night before you plan to start taping. If possible, have two charged power packs on hand.

3. ***Tripod vs. hand-held operation.*** A tripod is great for recording programs and activities confined to a specific location. It keeps the camera stable for quality taping. Hand-held operation is preferred when you must move around to get the right shots, and for almost all outdoor taping.

4. ***Varying the footage.*** For viewing variety, familiarize yourself with the zoom and wide-angle buttons. It's tough to compete with commercial productions (which change scenes, on average, once every 7 seconds), but you can give it a try. On the other hand, avoid too much movement or you'll make your audience dizzy.

5. ***Special features.*** Check out the camera's many special features, such as the fade and date/time buttons. They are easy to use and add a professional touch to your production. With some cameras, you can create title frames, captions, and so on.

6. ***Choosing the background.*** If possible, select or control background scenery or color to complement your project. It's worth it to move a program or activity or to create an appropriate background.

7. ***Controlling the length.*** If you have ever watched someone else's home videos or movies, and they seemed to go on forever, you know how important this is. Try to plan out in advance each scene you will tape. Stay conscious of your audience and what is most likely to hold their interest.

CREATE YOUR OWN VIDEOS

What can you do with a video camera? Following are some suggestions for events and activities worth taping:

- ▶ Skits and role plays
- ▶ Puppet shows
- ▶ Oral reports
- ▶ Demonstrations
- ▶ Interviews
- ▶ Group projects
- ▶ Lyceum programs (lectures, entertainments)
- ▶ Field trips and other special activities
- ▶ Lesson segments
- ▶ Special lessons, guest speakers

SHHHH!

If you'd like your students to work quietly, try walking around the room and videotaping individuals and groups while they work. Students tend to buckle down and work extra hard as the camera approaches. *Tip:* If you find that this has an opposite effect on your students—if they get distracted or more active and "clown" for the camera—stop immediately. The success of this technique depends on the chemistry and maturity of your classroom.

THE YEAR IN REVIEW

Tape a running documentary of classroom projects and activities titled "The Year in Review." Keep careful notes about what you film and make sure that *every* student in your class appears at least once. At the end of the year, make copies to give to your students. It's better than a yearbook!

AUDIO ADVENTURES

Inventive uses for cassette tapes, recorders, CDs, and albums

112 — TAPED LESSONS

Prerecord portions of your lesson on audiocassette. Turn the tape on and off when the timing is appropriate. Discuss what was shared on tape, or give your students time to catch up on taking notes. *Example:* Tape vocabulary and spelling words, definitions, and sentences using the words. Play the tape and stop it occasionally for clarification, discussion, or expansion.

113 — LISTEN CAREFULLY

Play a prerecorded message for the students covering such topics as lesson content, instructions, or any other information you feel is important. *Example:* "Good morning, boys, and girls! It's a wonderful day and I'm glad you are here with us to talk about...." Use the tape to introduce a lesson or later on to stimulate interest.

114 — SOUND EFFECTS & BACKGROUND MUSIC

Check your school's media center for background music and sound-effects tapes. Integrate selections into lessons, stories, and drama productions. Background music can also be used to set a specific mood. Slow, soft, soothing music creates a warm atmosphere. Loud, fast, rambunctious music is energizing. Using this technique can be as simple as turning on a tape during work times or lesson transitions. *Tip:* If you have an electronic keyboard, bring it to class. Many keyboards have built-in sound effects and music.

STUDENT ASSIGNMENTS 115

Select part of a text or a story that relates to a future lesson. Assign one or more students to prepare a tape recording of the material. They can do a straight reading or dress it up with voice impressions, sound effects, interviews, background music, etc. Build their recording into your lesson. *Example:* For a literature lesson on fables, you might assign a student to read a short fable to students on the playground, or to family members at home, then interview the "audience" to find out what they think the moral is. Use this student assignment to kick off your lesson in class.

SUBSTITUTE TEACHER 116

If you have a learning center in your classroom, use the tape recorder as a substitute teacher for small groups or as a tutor for individual instruction. Record specific instructions, content, or assignments. Provide headphone sets for the student(s). If several students will be using headphones simultaneously, you'll need a junction box (check with your school AV or media department).

TELEPHONE TAPING 117

Check your local electronics store for a simple, inexpensive device that attaches to the telephone for tape recording. Use it to record interviews or conversations. *Examples:* A student's interview of a local sports celebrity; a teacher's conversation with an expert in a specific field (the weather, nuclear power, etc.). *Important:* You MUST get permission from the person on the other end to record the interview or conversation. Explain that the recording will be shared with the class.

118 ═══ HELP! ═══

WITH GREAT SURPRISE — I LEAPED TO MY FEET!

Students who have difficulty writing stories, reports, or other assignments may benefit from being allowed to dictate them onto a tape recorder, then transcribe them onto paper later. You may want to help with the transcription or ask a student assistant—someone skilled at typing or word processing. Or listen to the tape and grade it "by ear."

119 ═══ CLASS LIBRARY ═══

Record important discussions, lectures, or presentations. Label the tapes and keep them in a class library. Invite students to use the tapes for review or research, to catch up on classes they missed, etc. Have them "check out" tapes by writing their name and the tapes they are taking on a sign-out sheet. If your students seem to enjoy this class library of audiocassettes, consider adding spoken books and other audio resources, also available for check-out.

120 ═══ THE COLLECTION ═══

Develop your own classroom collection of tapes or CDs. Use this audio resource center for various reasons throughout the year. *Examples:* just for fun; class rewards; creating an affective atmosphere; specific lesson elements.

GETTING STARTED

Anyone can learn to cartoon

This part of *TNT Teaching* includes start-up suggestions and techniques to try yourself and share with your students. These are followed by several pages of examples to copy, trace, or study. You may photocopy these examples and use them as handouts. Or create a complete class set for students to use whenever they like. Soon your classroom will come alive with animated drawings—on your worksheets, posters, bulletin boards, chalkboard, floors, ceilings, everywhere!

But first, you'll need to gather a few supplies....

Necessary:

1. Two black felt-tipped pens

2. Two #2 pencils

3. Soft eraser

4. Ruler

Optional:

1. Tool box or fishing box (with large storage compartments to hold pencils, markers, etc.)

2. Kneadable eraser (a gum-like eraser that stretches and doesn't leave any residue on the paper)

3. Pencils and markers in various skin tones

4. Watercolor markers

5. Colored pencils

6. Tempera paints

7. Crayons

8. White-out

9. Pocket mirror (to check out personal facial expressions)

TECHNIQUES FOR BEGINNERS

Easy tricks to try

DOTS & DASHES

121

You can use the simplest designs and patterns to communicate a variety of messages. It's amazing how many different facial expressions you can create with three dots and a dash. This is a key cartooning technique that anyone can master instantly.

KEEP IT SIMPLE

122

When you look at a good cartoon, you may wonder, "How did they do that? It looks so difficult!" But if you study how it was drawn, you'll see that it's nothing more than a collection of geometric shapes arranged in simple patterns. If you can draw squares, circles, and triangles, you have the potential to create successful cartoons. Start by sketching your basic shapes—squares, circles, triangles, stick figures, irregular shapes and patterns. Then start adding the details. Avoid adding too many details, since this may distract from the message and humor of your cartoon. You'll find several examples of this two-step process on the following page.

SHAPES & DETAILS

Which cartoon in each of these pairs looks more "cartoonish" and why? You'll probably answer "the one on the right" because the one on the left looks too lifelike. Cartoons by definition should include an element of humor. A simple way to achieve this is by exaggerating body parts and bodies. Make a big nose HUGE. Make a big person IMMENSE. Stretch, slant, overstate, and overemphasize any feature you choose. Political cartoonists are masters of this technique. Bring examples of political cartoons to class for your students to study.

LEFT   RIGHT

LEFT   RIGHT

LEFT   RIGHT

The eyes of a cartoon character set the mood, communicate the message, and reveal the character's personality. Look at these examples, then draw some eyes of your own.

happy

sad, sleepy

angry, mean

goofy, crazy

worried, embarrassed

scared, afraid

It's easy to make your eyes come to life. Just add little white dots. These imitate the way light reflects off of real eyes.

Which pair of eyes do you like better and why? Keep this in mind as you position the eyes in your cartoon characters' faces.

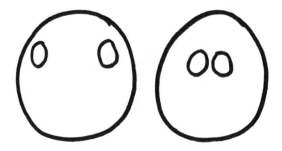

HEAD SHAPES

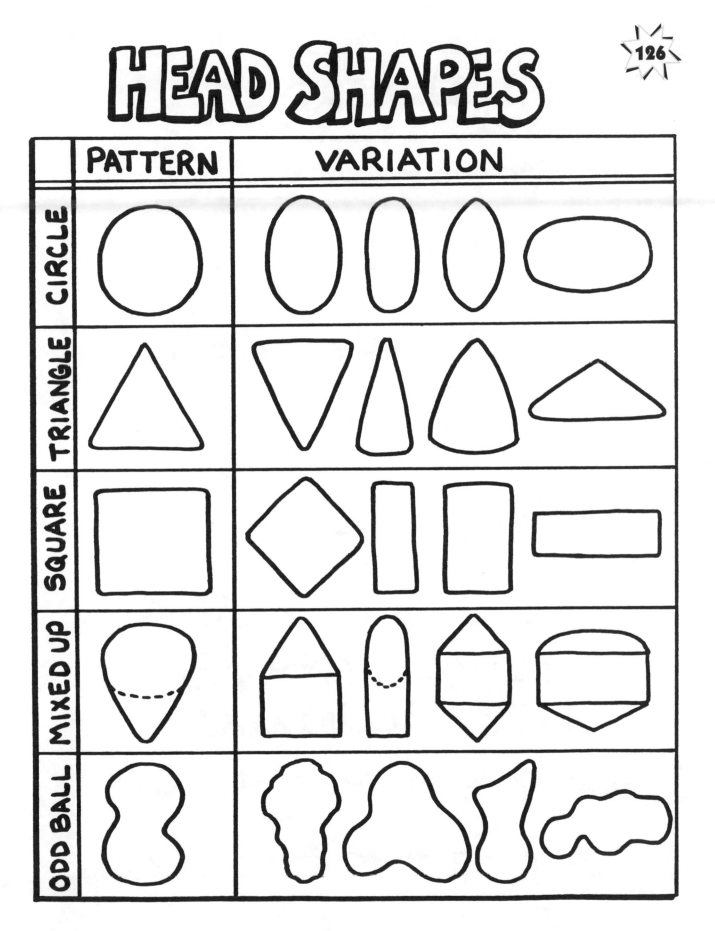

NOSES

FRONT VIEW

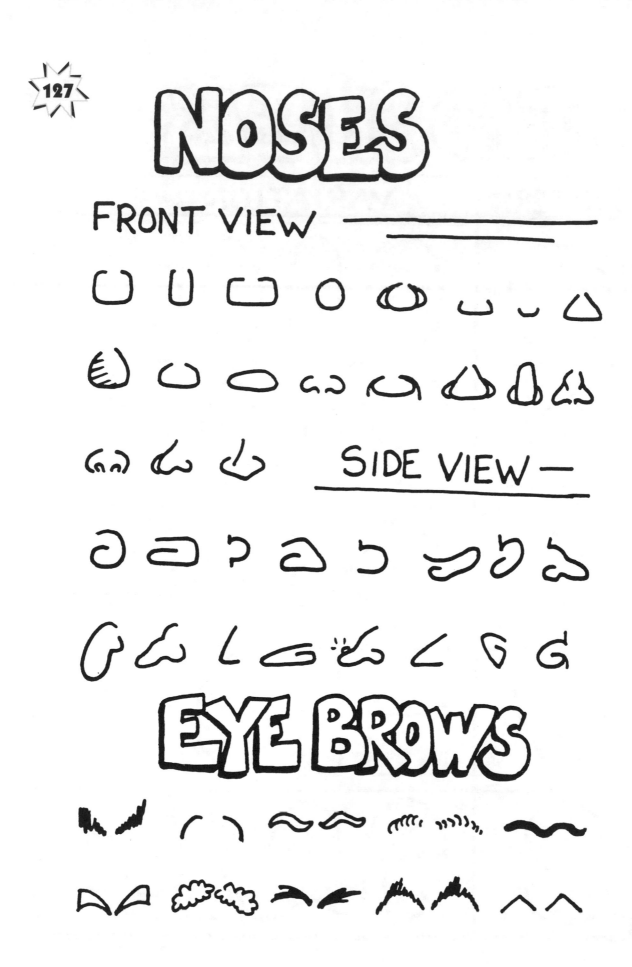

SIDE VIEW —

EYE BROWS

EYES

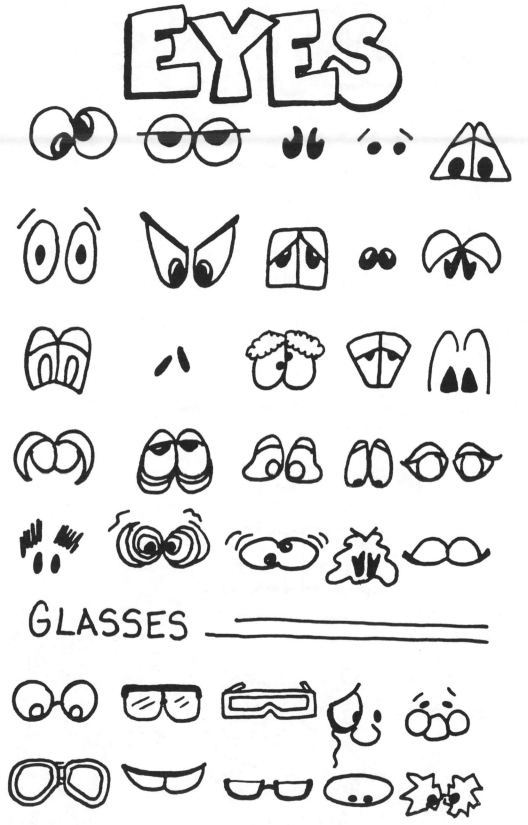

GLASSES

MOUTHS

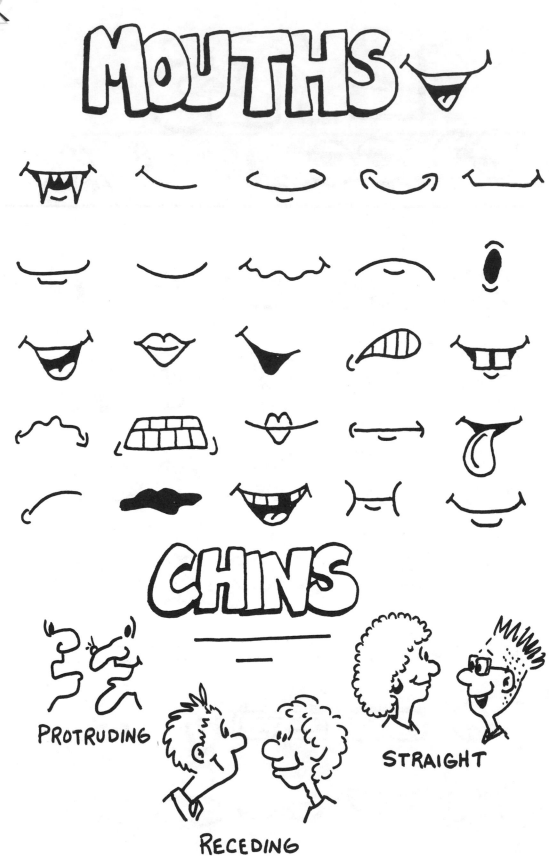

CHINS

PROTRUDING

RECEDING

STRAIGHT

EARS

MUSTACHES

BEARDS

TNT Teaching, copyright © 1994 Randy Moberg. Free Spirit Publishing Inc. Reproducible for classroom use only.

HAIRSTYLES

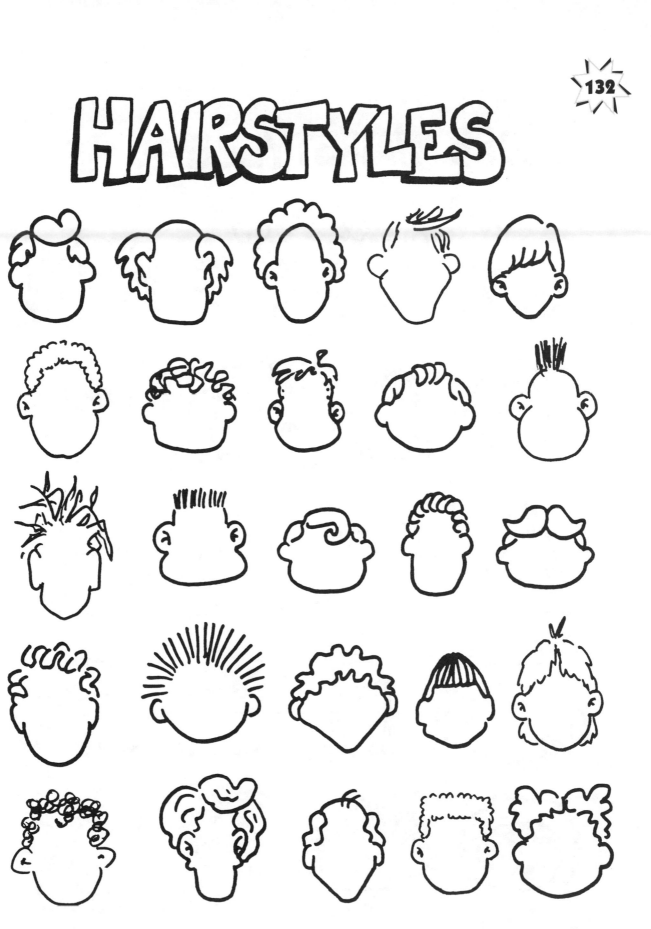

MORE HAIRSTYLES

HANDS

ACTION SHOTS

135

MORE ACTION SHOTS

BODY BLOCKS
FRONT VIEW

BODY BLOCKS - SIDE VIEW

75

TREES & SHRUBS

MORE TREES & SHRUBS

ANIMALS

MORE ANIMALS

VEHICLES

SPORTS EQUIPMENT

AROUND THE HOUSE

MORE AROUND THE HOUSE

CAPTION BALLOONS

BALLOON LETTERING

BALLOON LETTERING IS A VERSATILE TECHNIQUE THAT CAN ENHANCE YOUR ACTIVITY SHEETS, DISPLAYS, BULLETIN BOARDS, AND STUDENT PROJECTS. IT IS ALSO VERY EASY TO DO: JUST FOLLOW STEPS 1 AND 2. TRY EXPERIMENTING; BE CREATIVE WITH YOUR LETTER SHAPES.

STEP 1

STICK FIGURE

STEP 2

LETTER TRACING

• SHADE LEFT/BOTTOM FOR 3-D EFFECT

• ERASE STICK FIGURE LINES

OVERLAPPING LETTERS

WRITE WORDS IN STICK FORM. LETTERS WILL NATURALLY OVERLAP!

CHANGES OF SCENE

New views for your classroom

This section features an assortment of background scenery that can be used to accent any story written or performed by your students. These scenes can also enhance the lessons you teach. For example, if it happens to be a blazing hot day, you might choose the scene of the blazing sun...or the snowfall, to set a cooler mood. If you present a lesson about life in medieval times, you might use the castle scene. If there is a thunderstorm in your lesson (or outside), use the storm cloud scene. The key is to think about your lesson, the weather, current events, etc. and capitalize on this flexible visual medium. Following are several more suggestions for using fascinating backgrounds.

149 — SCREEN SCENES

Make a transparency of a scene, color it in with markers, and place it on the overhead projector. Small backdrops can be projected onto a movie screen. When you want full-wall scenes, back up the overhead projector to achieve the desired size. One problem with this format is that you cast a shadow on the scene, as part of it is projected directly on you. Eliminate this "zebra effect" by hanging a large white sheet in front of the room and projecting the scene from *behind* the sheet.

150 — GIANT MURALS

Make a transparency of a scene. Tape large pieces of white butcher paper to the wall. Project the transparency onto the paper and trace it with black permanent marker. Take it off the wall and paint it with tempera paints. Let it dry completely, then retrace with black permanent marker. Mount with heavy-duty tape and enjoy your giant mural.

151 — STORY STARTERS

These illustrations make great story starters for student writing activities. Make photocopies of one scene, pass them out, and have students write about it. Or give them several scenes and have them create stories using 4-5 pictures.

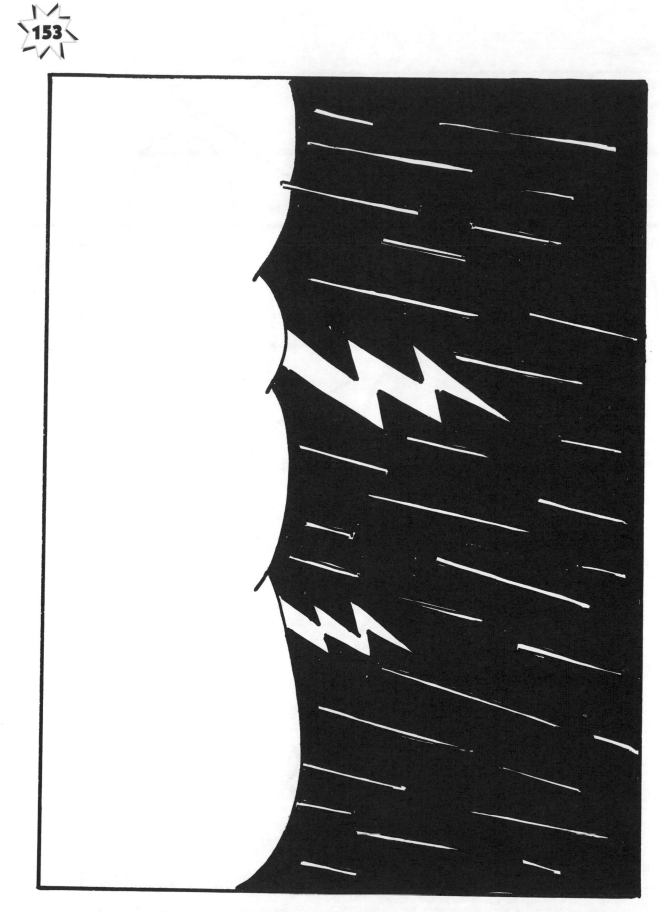

TNT Teaching, copyright © 1994 Randy Moberg. Free Spirit Publishing Inc. Reproducible for classroom use only.

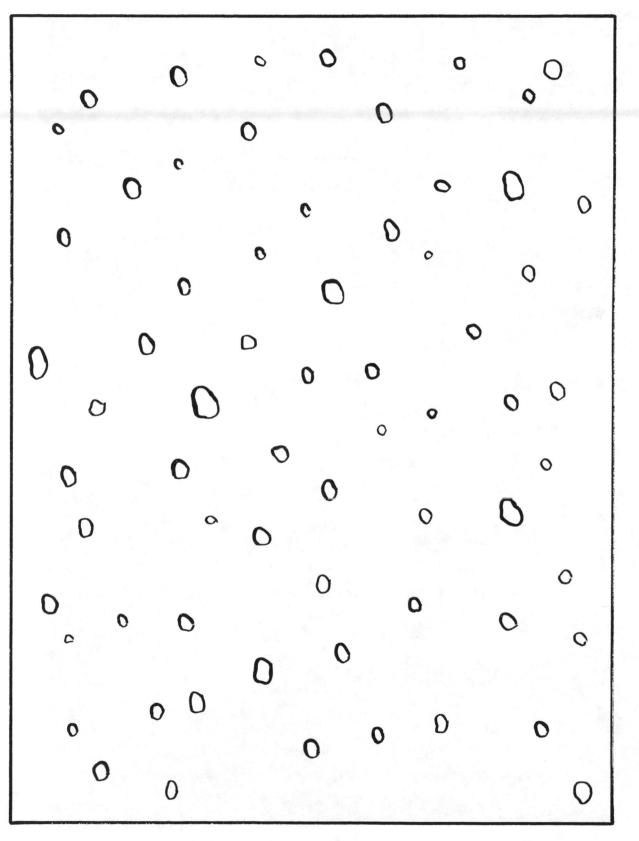

TNT Teaching, copyright © 1994 Randy Moberg. Free Spirit Publishing Inc. Reproducible for classroom use only.

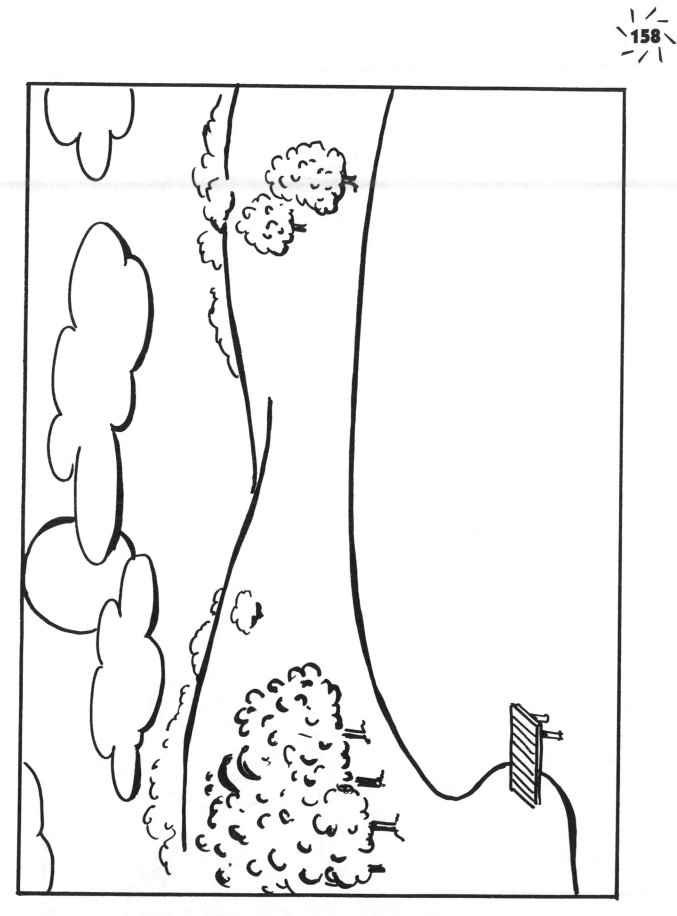

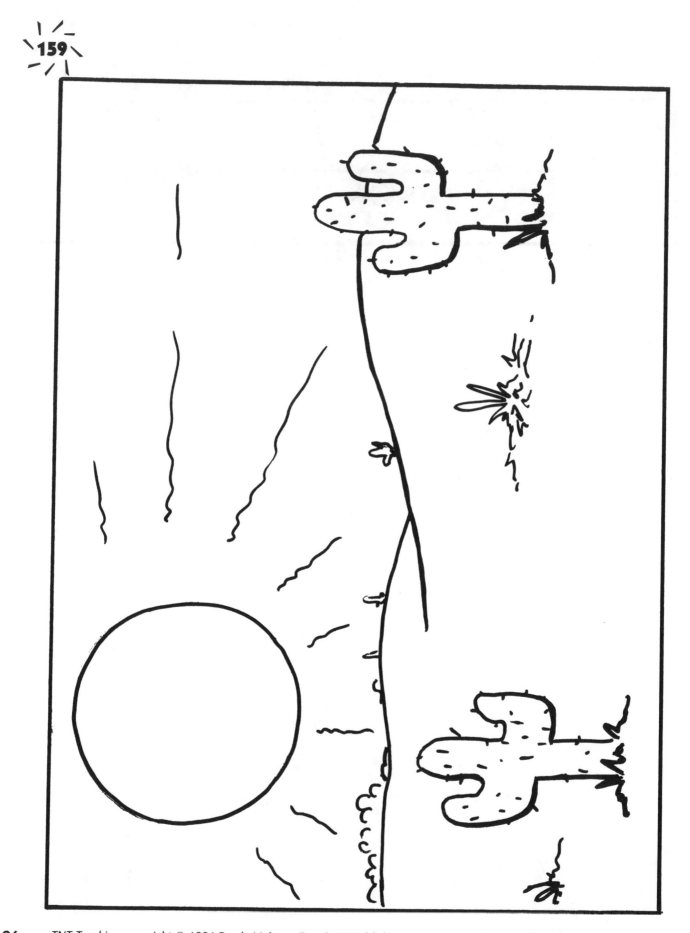

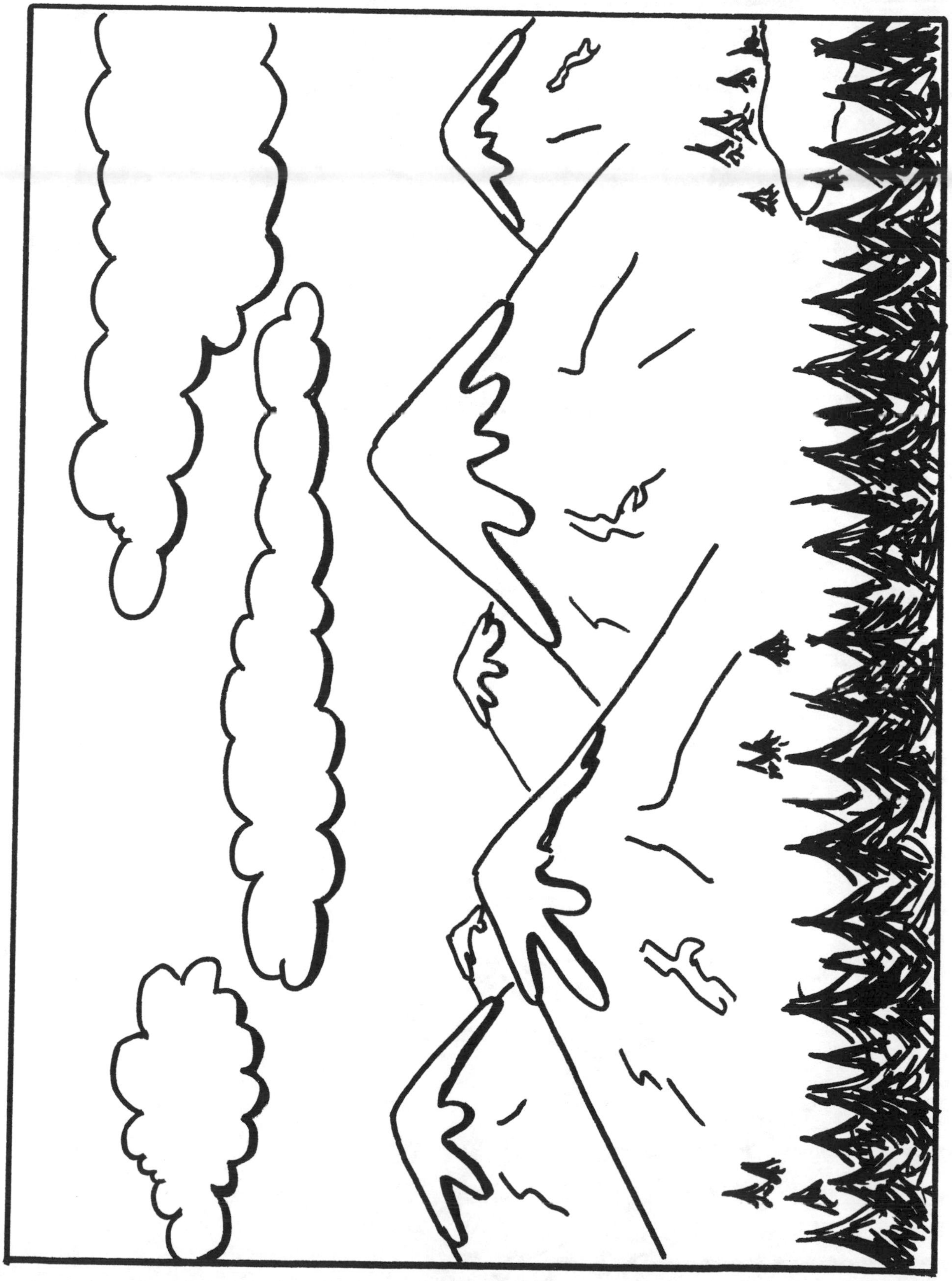

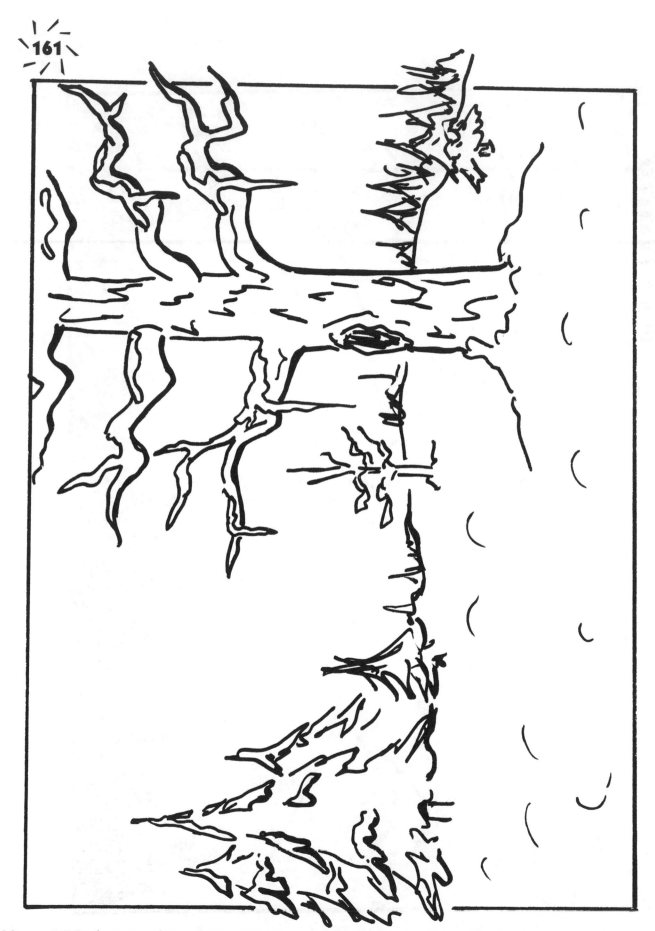

TNT Teaching, copyright © 1994 Randy Moberg. Free Spirit Publishing Inc. Reproducible for classroom use only.

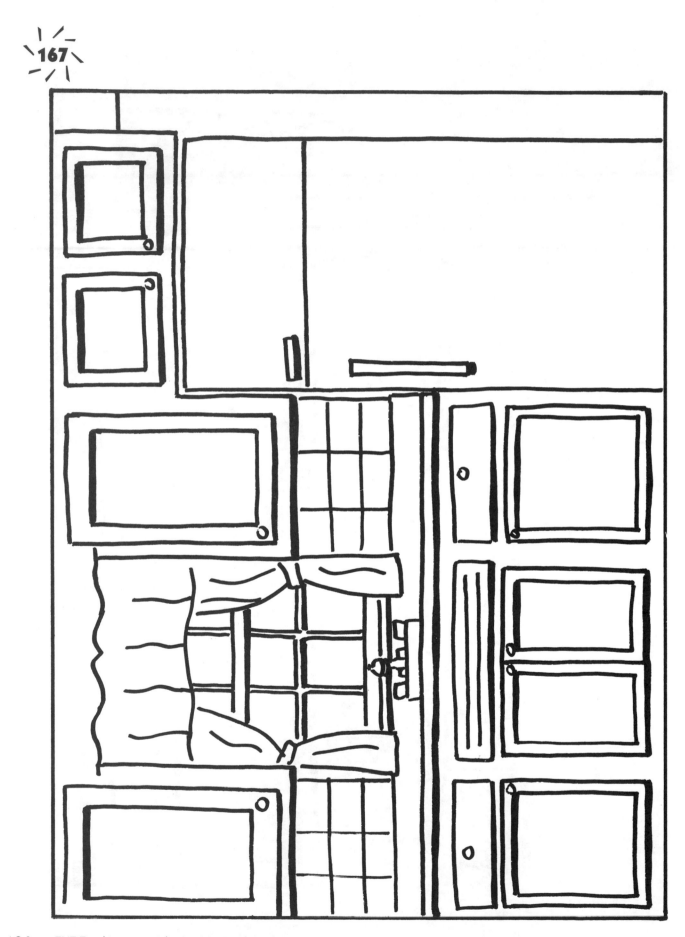

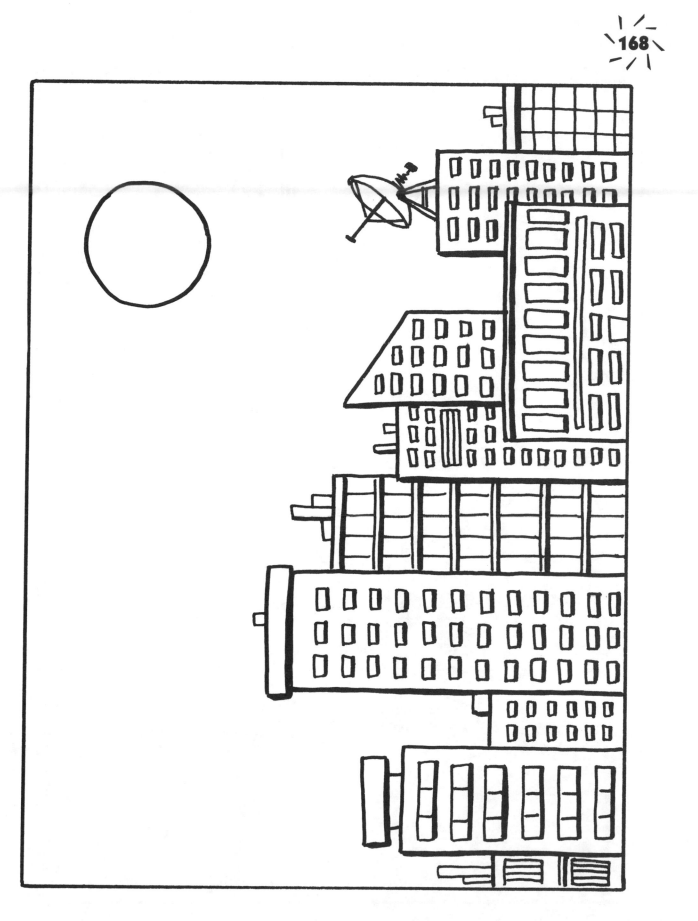

TNT Teaching, copyright © 1994 Randy Moberg. Free Spirit Publishing Inc. Reproducible for classroom use only.

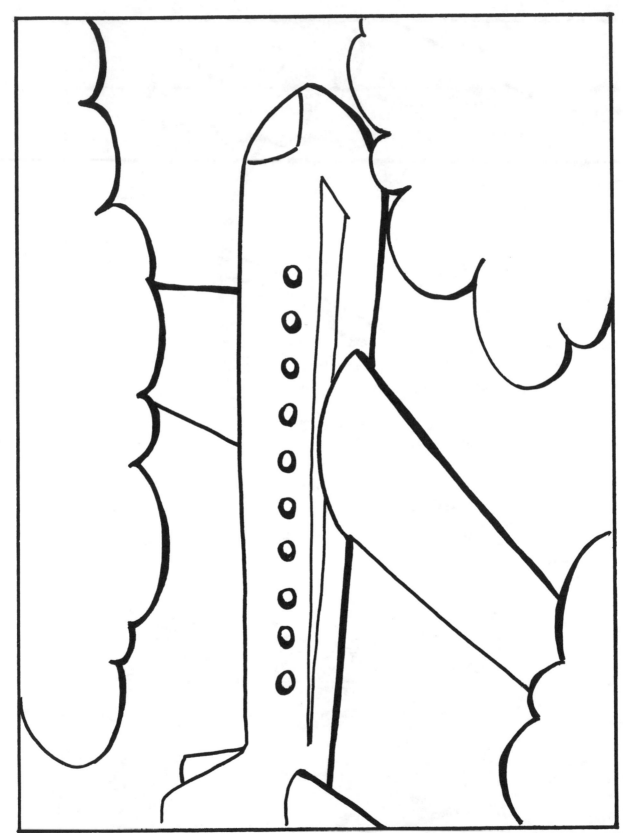

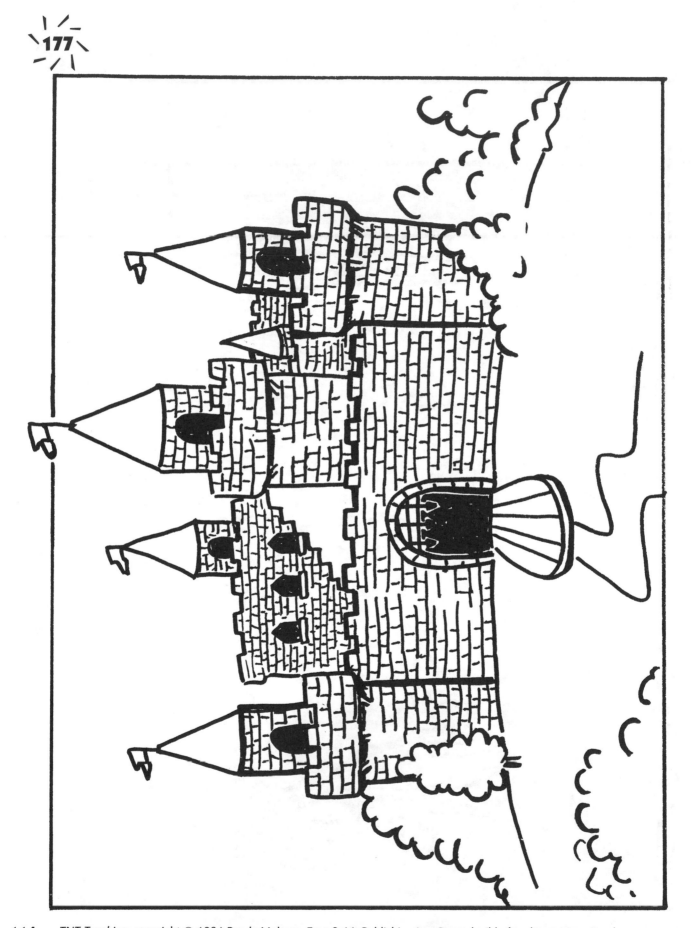

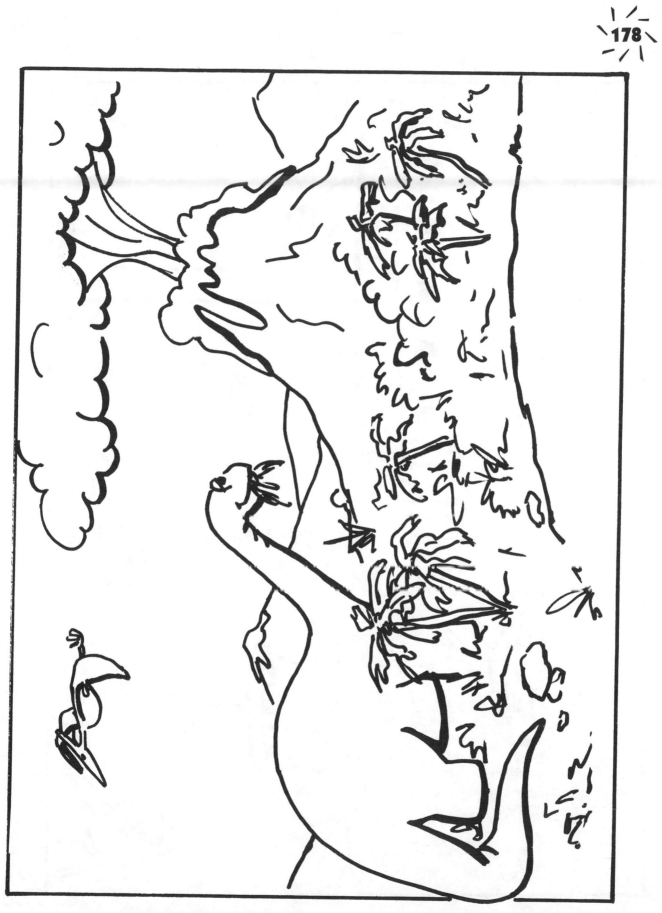

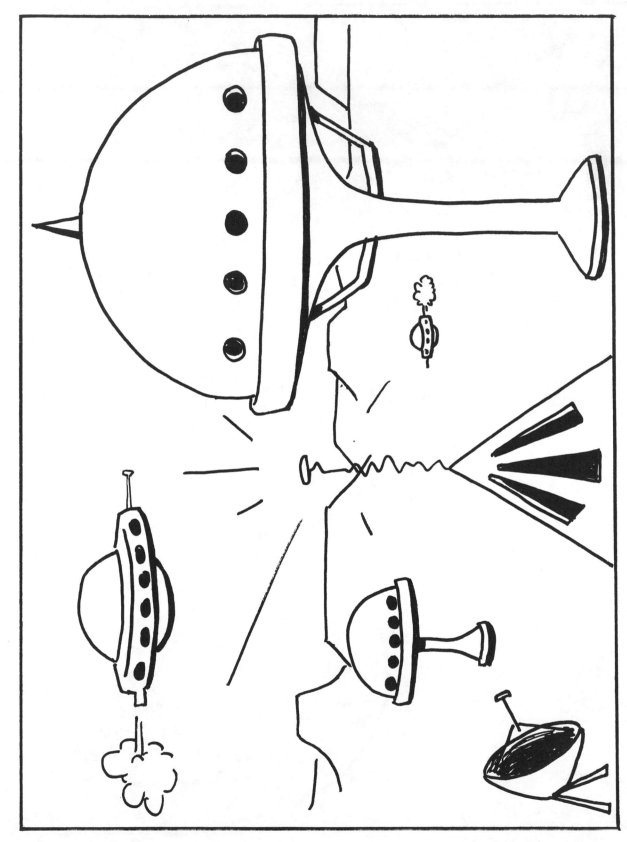

TNT Teaching, copyright © 1994 Randy Moberg. Free Spirit Publishing Inc. Reproducible for classroom use only.

THE ART OF SELF-EXPRESSION

When a picture is worth a thousand words

Language and art both express thoughts, moods, and feelings. They just do it in different ways—one in words and punctuation, the other in shapes and pictures. The framing kit in this section will help your students combine language and art to communicate a message. The pages may be used by students and teachers for a variety of educational purposes across the curriculum. *Tips:* Make several copies of each page to have on hand whenever you ask your students to do any writing and/or illustrating. Give your students the freedom to decide which they want to work on first, the writing or the picture. Many students use drawing as a pre-writing activity.

180 JOURNALING

Make framing pages available for journaling activities. You may want to hand out a different page for every journaling assignment (this section includes 14 possibilities—28 more if you also turn them upside down). Three-hole-punch them ahead of time so students can keep their completed pages in a notebook. At the end of the year, they will have a vivid record in words and pictures of the year's events.

181 ASSIGNMENTS & TESTS

Hand out framing pages whenever you ask your students to respond to a question or clarify their ideas about a particular topic. When they have the freedom to sketch an idea or two, they may think more clearly and creatively.

TEACHING TOOLS 182

Turn framing pages into overhead transparencies and use them to model assignments, write lesson outlines, or teach lesson concepts. Use the boxes for illustrations or diagrams during instruction.

POETRY WRITING 183

The framing kit is excellent for teaching poetry—reading or writing. Have students copy poems they are learning, then add their own illustrations. If your students are writing original poems, let them choose the pages they want for their final copies.

STORY WRITING 184

Let students use the framing kit to create original stories complete with illustrations. This encourages them to vary their picture placement on the page, which makes for a more polished final product. The storyline handout on page 120 will help them to create interesting stories. *Tip:* For elementary students, cut the framing pages In half.

BOOK PUBLISHING 185

Even reluctant writers enjoy creating their own books. The book format guide on page 121 suggests a general layout. Page 122 shows how the various framing pages can be combined in eye-catching layouts.

STORY Line

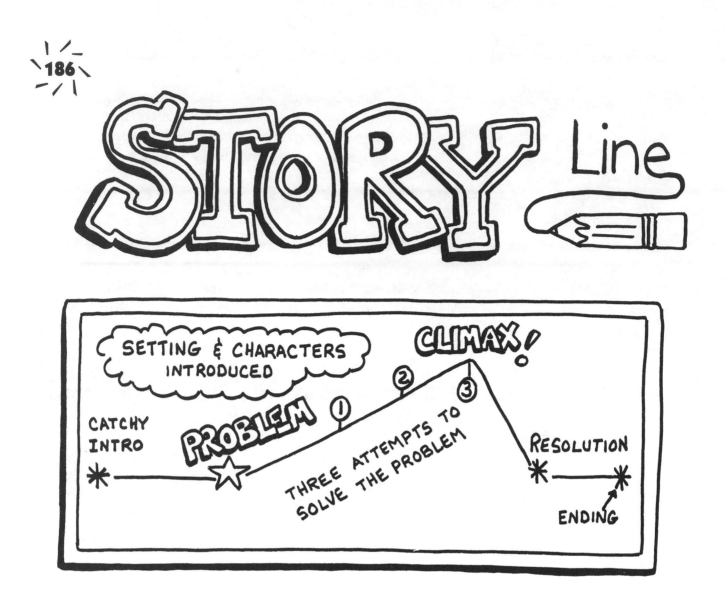

CATCHY INTRO – An interesting and appealing opening that will get the reader involved in the story.

SETTING – When and where the story takes place.

CHARACTERS – The people in the story. ("Characters" don't have to be people. Yours might be animals, aliens from another planet, etc.)

PROBLEM – The conflict that the major character(s) will face.

CLIMAX – The most exciting part of the story, where the problem is just about to be solved.

RESOLUTION – The part of the story where the problem is solved. This happens *quickly* during or right after the climax.

ENDING – An appropriate closure to the story.

BOOK FORMAT
A GENERAL LAYOUT GUIDE

FRONT COVER

▶ Title

▶ Illustration

▶ Author's name

▶ Illustrator's name

INSIDE FRONT COVER

A brief paragraph tells the reader what the story is about without giving away the ending. It gets the reader interested in wanting to read more.

FIRST PAGE

▶ Title

▶ Author's name

▶ Illustrator's name

▶ Dedication

▶ Publisher

▶ Year of copyright

STORY PAGES

Correct spelling and grammar errors *before* writing your final copy on framing pages. Write neatly. Add illustrations. Use a variety of framing pages for variety and interest. See the Story Page Layout Combinations sheet for ideas.

INSIDE BACK COVER

▶ Photo/illustration of author

▶ Interesting facts about author

▶ Photo/illustration of illustrator

▶ Interesting facts about illustrator

STORY PAGE LAYOUT COMBINATIONS

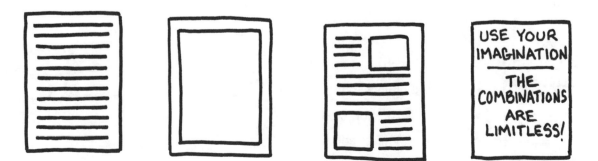

USE YOUR IMAGINATION

THE COMBINATIONS ARE LIMITLESS!

TNT Teaching, copyright © 1994 Randy Moberg. Free Spirit Publishing Inc. Reproducible for classroom use only.

TNT Teaching, copyright © 1994 Randy Moberg. Free Spirit Publishing Inc. Reproducible for classroom use only.

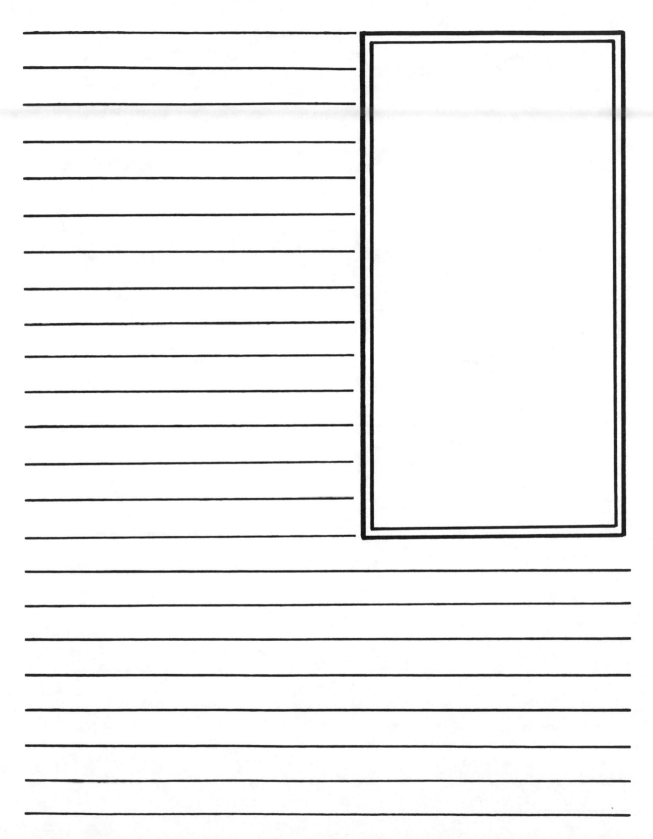

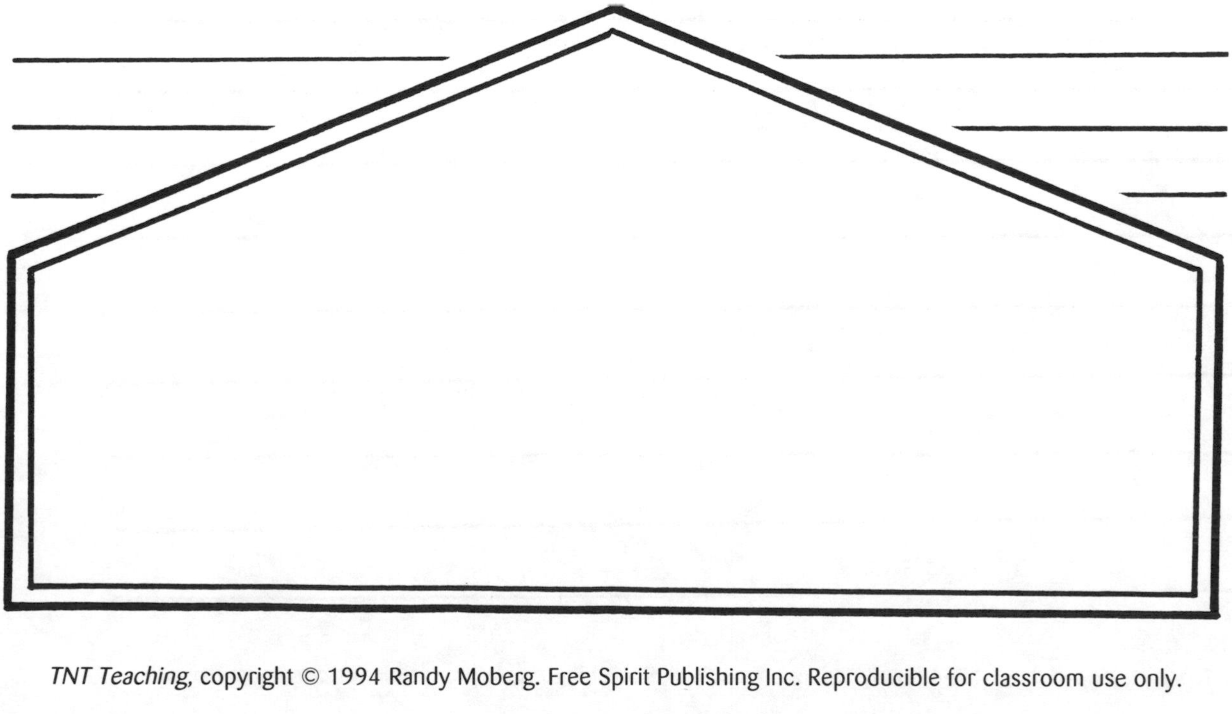

_____

_____

_____

_____

_____

_____

_____

_____

_____

_____

_____

_____

TNT Teaching, copyright © 1994 Randy Moberg. Free Spirit Publishing Inc. Reproducible for classroom use only.

_____

_____

_____

_____

_____

_____

_____

_____

_____

_____

_____

_____

_____

_____

_____

_____

_____

_____

_____

_____

_____

_____

_____

_____

_____

_____

_____

_____

_____

_____

_____

_____

_____

TNT Teaching, copyright © 1994 Randy Moberg. Free Spirit Publishing Inc. Reproducible for classroom use only.

GAMES PEOPLE PLAY

Create your own for review and fun

Games are a great way to share knowledge and review subject matter. It's easier than you may think to create original games for your classroom—especially if you invite your students to contribute their ideas and designs. This kit gets everyone involved in the exciting process of game creation. You'll start by designing generic game boards, then move on to developing complete games.

203 — GENERIC GAME BOARDS

Follow these steps:
1. INTRODUCE
   a. Introduce the unit objective: "To create a generic game board that can be used to review a variety of subjects."
   b. Brainstorm types of board games currently available.
   c. Have students bring board games to class.
2. EXPERIMENT
   a. Divide the class into groups of 3-4 students.
   b. Play the board games.
   c. Document and discuss each game's strengths and weaknesses.
3. CREATE
   a. Review the unit objective; make sure everyone understands what they will be doing.
   b. Distribute materials needed to create game boards. *Tip:* Clean pizza boxes work well, plus you can store game pieces inside. Check with a local pizzeria.
4. EVALUATE
   a. Play and evaluate each game board at least once.
   b. Give each group a final grade.

204 — NEW GAMES

Once your students have designed and tested their generic game boards, they may be ready for a new challenge: designing complete original games. As with the generic game board project, the overall objective should be to create a game that can be used to review subject material. But this time students can *choose* their subject. Some might create science or math games; others might prefer to work on literature or history games. Divide the class into groups or let students form their own groups. Distribute copies of the Game Kit to each group, establish a time frame and schedule, and be available for questions. The Game Kit includes the Game Plan handout, the Game Plan Flow Chart, the New Game Proposal form, the Question Tips handout, and the About This Game form, all found on the following pages.

GAME PLAN

12 STEPS FOR CREATING A NEW REVIEW GAME

Note: The Game Plan Flow Chart summarizes these steps.

1. Decide on the subject of your game. Will it be a math challenge? A literature review? A science game? It's up to you.

2. Choose a theme for your game. *Examples:* sports, space, animals, TV programs, famous people.

3. Determine the object of your game. *Examples:* To answer 5 questions correctly; to be the first to reach the "Winner's Circle;" to beat the clock; to win the most money (design your "dollar bills" in various denominations—$1, $5, $20, $50, $100); etc. For ideas, study other games. Most include a statement somewhere in the introduction or the rules about "the object of the game."

4. Brainstorm game ideas. Make sure that the main focus of your game stays on reviewing subject matter or sharing knowledge. Your game should be fun to play, but with a purpose.

5. Come up with a name for your game.

6. Write a description of your game. *Tip:* Keep it short and simple—one paragraph should be enough.

7. Fill out a New Game Proposal form and turn it in to your teacher for approval. Your teacher may have comments and suggestions about your game. You may want to rethink your game, make some changes, and write up another Game Proposal form for approval.

8. Create a "rough draft" of your game.

   a. Make a full-size sketch of your game board on paper. Number or label each area. Build in an element of chance or luck—include spaces where players must move ahead or back, miss a turn, etc.

   b. Decide how players will move around your game board. *Examples:* dice, coins, cards, spinner. If you use a spinner, include spaces with an element of chance or luck.

   c. Create the questions for your game. See the Question Tips handout for help.

   d. Write the rules for your game. At this stage, it's okay to just jot down some ideas; as your game takes shape, your rules might change, so save the final rules for the end. *Tip:* Keep them simple!

9. Play a few turns of your game and do a preliminary evaluation. Are the questions interesting? Is it easy and fun to move around the board? Is this a game you and your friends would enjoy playing? Is the main focus on reviewing subject matter or sharing knowledge? Make any changes needed to improve your game.

10. Create the final version of your game.

    a. Draw your game board on cardboard or tagboard. To make your game board foldable (and easier to store), use 2 or 4 smaller pieces of cardboard or tagboard taped together at the seams.

    b. Illustrate your game board by hand, with pictures cut from magazines, or with computer graphics.

    c. Collect or create the pieces you need—playing pieces, dice or spinner, etc.

    d. Write your questions on slips of paper or 3" x 5" index cards. Write the answer on the back of each question or create a separate answer key.

    e. Complete an About This Game sheet to include with your finished game.

11. Create a durable, practical, space-efficient way to store your game, including small pieces. *Examples:* An old box for a game you no longer use; a shoebox (if your game board can be folded); a plastic bin; a pizza box; a storage box you design and build, complete with dividers.

12. Play and enjoy your game. Ask for feedback; you may want to make a few changes to the rules, for example, or modify your game board in some way that improves it.

GAME PLAN FLOW CHART

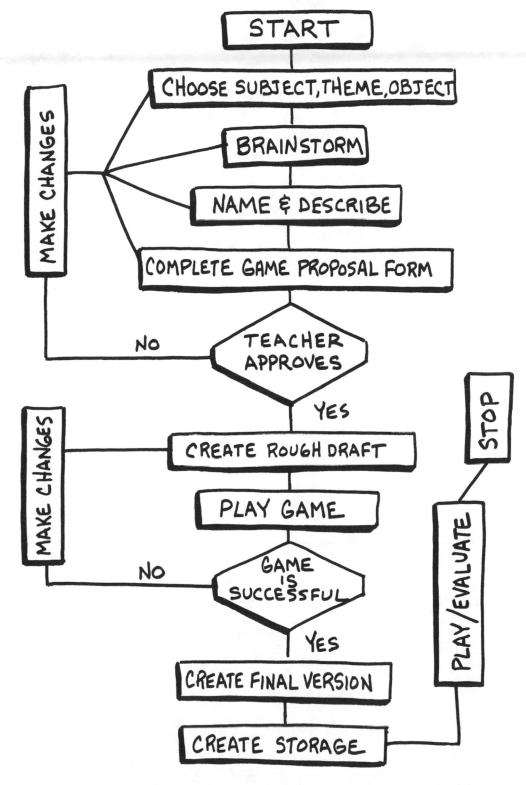

START

CHOOSE SUBJECT, THEME, OBJECT

BRAINSTORM

NAME & DESCRIBE

COMPLETE GAME PROPOSAL FORM

MAKE CHANGES

TEACHER APPROVES — NO

YES

CREATE ROUGH DRAFT

MAKE CHANGES

PLAY GAME

GAME IS SUCCESSFUL — NO

YES

CREATE FINAL VERSION

CREATE STORAGE

PLAY/EVALUATE

STOP

207

NEW GAME PROPOSAL

Game Designers: ______________________

____

____

____

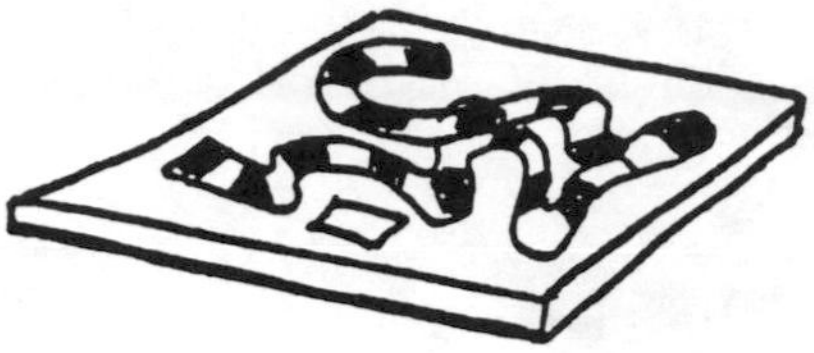

The Name of the Game: ______________________

The Object of the Game: ______________________

____

____

Rough Sketch of Game Board

Brief Description of the Game: ______________________

____

____

____

____

Game questions can be like quiz or test questions. Choose one of the following forms for your game questions, or mix-and-match for more variety.

1. FILL-IN-THE-BLANK

Example:

_____ is the President of the United States.

2. TRUE OR FALSE

Example:

Earth is the fifth planet from the Sun. True or false?

3. MULTIPLE CHOICE

Example:

The most important international, national, and local stories in a newspaper are found:

a. in the entertainment section

b. on the editorial page

c. on the front page

4. SHORT ANSWER

Example:

Water is steam in the gaseous state. What is water in the solid state?

5. OPEN-ENDED (questions with more than one possible right answer)

Example:

What are some of the effects the Civil War had on the United States?

Tip: Your answer key should include at least three possible answers for every open-ended question.

6. OPINION

Example:

What do you think about...? How do you feel about...?

Tip: Answers to opinion questions are *always* right answers.

ABOUT THIS GAME

Name of game: _____

Created by: _____

_____

_____

_____

Created on: _____

month, date, year

Number of players: _____

What this game includes (board, questions, pieces, etc.):

_____

_____

_____

The object of this game is to:

_____

_____

_____

Game rules:

_____

_____

_____

_____

_____

_____

_____

_____

_____

How to start the game:

_____

_____

_____

_____

_____

The game is over when:

_____

_____

_____

_____

_____

Hints and tips:

_____

_____

_____

_____

_____

_____

Anything else players should know to enjoy this game

_____

_____

_____

_____

_____

_____

_____

GAME EVALUATION

Name of game: _____

Players: _____

Please mark the scales and answer the questions.

1. How much did you enjoy playing the game?
   (5 = very much, 1 = you didn't enjoy it)

   5   4   3   2   1

2. How clear were the instructions and rules?
   (5 = very clear, 1 = very confusing)

   5   4   3   2   1

3. How would you rate the parts of the game?
   (5 = excellent, 1 = needs improvement)

   a. Game board

       5   4   3   2   1

   b. Questions

       5   4   3   2   1

   c. Pieces

       5   4   3   2   1

   d. Other: _____

       5   4   3   2   1

4. How well does the game review the subject matter?
   (5 = very well, 1 = not very well)

   5   4   3   2   1

6. Did you learn anything new from playing this game?

   ☐ Yes ☐ No

7. Would you want to play this game again?

   ☐ Yes ☐ No

8. Give this game a final rating.
   (5 = excellent, 1 = needs improvement)

   5   4   3   2   1

9. Any other comments?

   _____

   _____

BEYOND THE RED PEN

New ways to correct student papers

If you're tired of lugging piles of student papers home for correcting...if you're weary of spending your lunch hour with red pen in hand...if you're bored with coming in early or staying late to handle the Paper Pile-up...this section of *TNT Teaching* is especially for you. Here you'll find fun and creative alternatives to the usual way of correcting student papers. They're easy to learn, fun to do, and they get your students involved.

211 ◼ STAR SEARCH ◼

Tell students to stand and have them correct the assignment orally by answering the questions in turn. Anyone who gives a wrong answer sits down. The last student standing is the winner of "Star Search." *Tip:* Use this technique with caution and good judgment. Remember that you want *all* students to feel successful.

212 ◼ THE GAMBLER ◼

Ask for a volunteer to correct the assignment orally. A wrong answer "loses the bet." The student must then do a silly stunt, described in advance by you. *Examples:* Jump up and down five times; quack like a duck; wear a silly hat for the rest of the day. The point of this is to have fun, never to shame the student, so make sure that everyone understands this in advance and nobody teases the student who "loses the bet."

213 ◼ FAIR EXCHANGE ◼

Tell students that when you ring a bell (or make some other prearranged sound), they are to pass their papers to the right and keep passing until you ring the bell again. They will correct the paper they are holding when they hear the second bell. Read the answers aloud to the class.

VARYING VOICE ➤ 214

Use a special tone (or tones) of voice for reading corrections. Try different dialects. Shout the answers or whisper them. Anything different will get your students' attention and make correcting more entertaining.

ANSWER CHORUS ➤ 215

At times it may be appropriate to have the whole class chant the answers. This works well with fill-in-the-blank, multiple choice, and true-or-false questions. Obviously it won't work with open-ended questions.

CODED CORRECTING ➤ 216

Invent special class symbols to take the place of standard correcting marks. *Example:* if you usually use an X to indicate a wrong answer and a checkmark to indicate a right answer, you might try a circle for a wrong answer and a star for a right answer—or anything else you choose. The symbols don't have to make sense as long as the whole class understands them.

POINTER POWER ➤ 217

Instead of calling out the answers when correcting student papers, put them on the overhead. Or make transparencies for multiple choice questions (A-B-C-D) and true-or-false questions (T or F) and use a pointer to indicate the right answer.

THE NAME GAME ➤ 218

When correcting multiple choice and true-or-false questions, give each letter a special name. *Examples:* "A" might become "Alex" or "Alice," "T" could be "Trudy" or "Terrell." Use the same names whenever you correct student papers or change them whenever you or your students want to.

LISTEN TO THE MUSIC ➤ 219

Gather a variety of instruments—rattle, bells, wooden sticks, xylophone, tambourine—or use your electronic keyboard. Play a note or two in between each answer. Or play one note for right answers, another for wrong answers.

INDEX

ABOUT THE AUTHOR

"There are two words I live my life by," Randy Moberg says. "Passion and compassion. I have a passion for my profession, and compassion for kids. I love what I'm doing."

Randy Moberg is the Gifted and Talented Specialist at Palmer Lake Elementary School in Brooklyn Park, Minnesota, where he works with grades K–6 and is an assistant to the principal. He also serves as the Children's Director in charge of special ministries at Redeemer Covenant Church in Brooklyn Park. He received his B.A. and M.A. in Education from the University of Minnesota.

He enjoys doodling, biking, reading, and playing basketball...but most of all, he loves spending time with his family. He and his wife, Melissa, have three sons, Joshua, Tyler, and Michael. They all live in Maple Grove with their dog, Molly; their rabbit, Rascal; and their bird, Kirby, named after Minnesota Twins star Kirby Puckett.

Randy is available for speeches, seminars, and workshops on the techniques described in *TNT Teaching*. Please contact him c/o Free Spirit Publishing Inc., 400 First Avenue North, Suite 616, Minneapolis, MN 55401; (612) 338-2068.